The Will of God
Past and Present

William Henry
&
Michael Penny

ISBN 978-1-78364-435-3

THE OPEN BIBLE TRUST
Fordland Mount, Upper Basildon,
Reading, RG8 8LU, UK.

www.obt.org.uk

The Will of God
Past and Present

In the Bible
& the 21st century

Publications of The Open Bible Trust must be in accordance with its evangelical, fundamental and dispensational basis. However, beyond this minimum, writers are free to express whatever beliefs they may have as their own understanding, provided that the aim in so doing is to further the object of The Open Bible Trust. A copy of the doctrinal basis is available on **www.obt.org.uk** or from:

THE OPEN BIBLE TRUST
Fordland Mount, Upper Basildon,
Reading, RG8 8LU, UK.

Contents

Page

About the authors

William Henry was born in Glasgow in 1949. He qualified as a Chartered Accountant and worked in the accountancy profession before entering academia, where he spent 25 years in teaching and research. At present he is an education consultant working with undergraduate and postgraduate students. He lives in Glasgow with his wife and two daughters.

Other publications by William Henry include: *No Condemnation – Romans 5:12-8:39; That you may know – 1 John; The Greatness of Christ; The Speeches in Acts; By Faith Abraham; The Making of the Man of God; Imitating Christ; The Signs in John's Gospel.*

He is an international speaker and has spoken in Canada, Australia and the Netherlands. He has recorded a number of Bible studies on CD and details of these, and the above publications, can be seen at **www.obt.org.uk**

William Henry and Michael Penny have also written

Following Philippians

which is ideal for Post-Alpha groups.

Details of this book can be seen on page 219 and on www.obt.org.uk

---

Michael Penny was born in Ebbw Vale, Gwent, Wales in 1943. He read Mathematics at the University of Reading, before teaching for twelve years and becoming the Director of Mathematics and Business Studies at Queen Mary's College Basingstoke in Hampshire, England. In 1978 he entered Christian publishing, and in 1984 became the administrator of The Open Bible Trust.

He held this position for seven years, before moving to the USA and becoming pastor of Grace Church in New Berlin, Wisconsin. He returned to Britain in 1999, and is at present the Administrator and Editor of The Open Bible Trust. In 2010 he was elected Chairman of Churches Together in Reading, where he speaks in a number of churches of different denominations. He is also a member of the Advisory Committee to Reading University Christian Union and ios a chaplain at Reading College.. He lives near Reading with his wife and has appeared on BBC Radio Berkshire and Premier Radio a number of times. He has made several speaking tours of America, Canada, Australia, New Zealand and the Netherlands, as well as others to South Africa and the Philippines. Some of his writings have been translated into German and Russian.

As well as writing articles for *Search* magazine and many Bible study booklets, he has also written several major books including: *The Manual on the Gospel of John; 40 Problem Passages; Approaching the Bible; Galatians - Interpretation and Application; The Miracles of the Apostles; Introducing God's Word* (with Carol Brown and Lynn Mrotek); *Introducing God's Plan* (with Sylvia Penny).

Details of these books, and other writings and recordings, can be seen at
www.obt.org.uk

It is imperative in the study of any subject to consider *all* that the Bible has to say.

This we have attempted to do by starting in Genesis and working our way through the Bible chronologically.

We have also paid attention to when new aspects of the will of God appear, and to when they change.

In the New Testament, we have also taken special care to distinguish between the will of God for Jews and His will for Gentiles. Sometimes it is the same ... but not always.

The Will of God: Past and Present

Introduction

Over the years we have spoken in many churches and at conferences throughout Britain and overseas. We have always encouraged questions and debate, and one of the subjects which continually crops up is that of the will of God. We have discovered that this is an issue for all Christians – young and mature alike. We live in a society where all are required to make many lifestyle choices and so Christians of all ages often wonder if they have made the 'right' decisions. Was what they decided to do the will of God?

As a result of this, in 2006 The Open Bible Trust published a small booklet called *The Clear Will of God*, looking solely at passages in the Bible which contained such expressions as 'the Will of God' or 'the Lord's will'. This proved to be the most popular booklet ever published by the OBT and it sold out in less than six months. A second printing the following year again sold out.

In 2009 the subject of three OBT conferences was *The Will of God in the 21st Century*. For these we expanded the material in that small booklet, going wider and into more detail. Again these proved popular and there was a great deal of discussion after each of the sessions.

We are grateful to all those people who questioned what we said and who contributed different points of view, and this book has tried to take into account the comments and questions raised at the conferences. Since then we have continued to study this subject, discuss it with others and debate it between ourselves.

The Will of God is an enormous subject and in this book we will not attempt to cover every aspect of it. There are a number of ways of looking at the Will of God; theologians often distinguish between God's *decretal* will and God's *preceptual* will:

God's decretal will

God's *decretal* will is what He decrees will happen. He is sovereign and His purposes will not be thwarted. An example of this is in Ephesians 1, where Paul speaks of the "mystery of his will" to bring all things in heaven and on earth together under one head, the Lord Jesus Christ. This dimension of His will is destined to come to pass. As Paul says in the same chapter:

> In him we were also chosen, having been predestined according to the plan of him who works out everything in conformity with the purpose of his will. (Ephesians 1:11)

God's preceptual will

On the other hand, God's *preceptual* will is to do with how He wants us to live. Sadly, our ignorance, or our refusal to follow His ways, may prevent His *preceptual* will from becoming a reality. This is the aspect of God's will that Paul wrote about in Ephesians 5:17:

> Therefore do not be foolish, but understand what the Lord's will is.

The Lord wants us to understand His will and then follow it. It is this *preceptual* will that concerns most Christians and it is this aspect of God's will that we will be considering in this book.

So ... What is it that God wants us to do? What sort of people does He want us to be in the world of the twenty-first century? What sort of lives should we live? Has His *preceptual* will, and the way He reveals it, remained the same over time?

The main source of information about the will of God is, of course, contained within the Bible, so our approach has been to examine what it has to say on the subject. We have attempted to explore the teaching on God's *preceptual* will throughout Scripture. We have considered changing circumstances and different stages of the progressive revelation of His purposes. This includes taking particular note as to whether a specific passage concerns Jews or Gentiles. Having studied God's *preceptual* will throughout the Bible, we finally turn our attention to some of the implications and possibilities for the twenty-first century.

Thus the book falls into three main sections:

1. The Will of God in the Old Testament

2. The Will of God in the New Testament

3. Implications and possibilities for the 21st century

It is our prayer that this book will provide an understanding of the ways in which the Lord revealed His will to His people down through the centuries and that it will help us to see which aspects of that *preceptual* will have changed and which have remained constant. We pray particularly that it will provide a clearer view of the Lord's will for the members of His body living in the 21st century world and of how He wants His people to live.

William Henry

Michael Penny

Section 1

God's revelation of His will

in the Old Testament

Chapter 1
Introduction

As in all aspects of the Judeo-Christian faith, it is very helpful to look at the Old Testament first to trace the way God has revealed His will for the human beings He has created. With the passage of time the cumulative revelation of God's nature and His will for mankind grew, and the methods by which He made His will known developed. As more of the Scriptures came to be written, there was less emphasis on direct interaction between God and specific individuals and more reliance on the written Word. God's revelation of Himself over time has been characterised by step changes brought about by specific events:

- the call of Abram, introducing God's sovereign purpose of blessing the world through a special nation;
- the giving of the Law at Sinai and after, establishing the Lord's will for Israel's worship and conduct;
- the coming of the Lord Jesus into the world, when the Word became flesh and revealed the Father and His ways in much clearer focus, with the subsequent writing of the Gospel records.
- the coming of the Holy Spirit at Pentecost as a permanent indwelling power in the life of the believer;
- the ministry of the apostles, recorded in Acts and the early epistles as the Lord expressed His will for the Jewish Christians and the increasing number of Gentile believers who were being brought into the Acts-period church;
- the setting aside of Israel at the end of Acts and the subsequent ministry of the apostle Paul.

It is therefore important for us to approach this subject chronologically. This will enable us to see how the Lord has revealed His will and to note the kind of issues that He emphasises, so that we can live according to the pattern He has laid down.

So when we come to the Old Testament, to see what it reveals about God's will, it is helpful to split this into the time before the giving of the Law and the time after that, because the introduction of the Law of Moses raised the extent of God's revelation of Himself to a new level.

Chapter 2

God's revelation of His will before the giving of the Law

Adam to Babel – God's will for particular individuals

In the early chapters of Genesis we read that Adam was given a stewardship responsibility over the Garden of Eden, to "work it and take care of it" (Genesis 2:15), a task which included the naming of "all the livestock, the birds of the air and all the beasts of the field." (Genesis 2:20). God seems to have had the habit of walking in the garden in the cool of the day and talking with Adam and Eve, discussing what they were doing. Presumably He would tell them His will on specific issues during these times, but Genesis does not mention this.

However, Adam was given one particular command – not to eat the fruit of the tree of the knowledge of good and evil, on pain of death. This, of course, proved to be his undoing and after they disobeyed the Lord, Adam and Eve hid from Him and the intimate relationship was lost.

In the aftermath of the expulsion from the Garden, God *occasionally* interacted directly with mankind – for example in confronting Cain about his offering and the subsequent murder of Abel. However, the relationship was broken and regular communication from God appears to have ceased until the time of Noah.

In the meantime, with God's silence, man's degeneration appears to have been given free rein. We read that:

> The Lord saw how great man's wickedness on the earth had become, and that every inclination of the thoughts of his heart was only evil all the time... the earth was corrupt in God's sight and was full of violence. (Genesis 6:5,11)

Mankind had become so corrupt that God decided to wipe them off the face of the earth (Genesis 6:7).

However, Noah was righteous and walked with God (Genesis 6:9) and God expressed His will to him in relation to a very specific project – the building of the ark. The Lord guided Noah through the building work, the collecting of the animals and entry into the ark. When he eventually emerged after the flood God again revealed His will for Noah and established His covenant with him. In Genesis 9, there are four distinct instructions which God gave to Noah and his family:

1. *Be fruitful and fill the earth*: Here the Lord was repeating His instructions to Adam and Eve in Genesis 1:28, although the instruction to "subdue" the earth was not repeated.

2. *Start eating meat as well as green plants*: In Genesis 1:29 God gave every seed-bearing plant and every fruit tree to Adam as food. In Genesis 9 God supplemented Noah's diet with meat.

> "Everything that lives and moves will be food for you. Just as I gave you the green plants, I now give you everything." (Genesis 9:3)

The relationship between man and animals had now changed.

> The fear and dread of you will fall upon all the beasts of the earth and all the birds of the air, upon every creature that moves along the ground, and upon all the fish of the sea; they are given into your hands. (Genesis 9:2)

This is hardly surprising if they are likely to be eaten! But there is one proviso:

3. *Do not eat blood:* In Genesis 9:4 Noah was forbidden to eat meat with the lifeblood in it – a forerunner of one of the terms of the Mosaic Law, which is observed by many Jews to this day.

In addition, there was an important requirement for human society:

4. *Every man will be accountable for his fellow man:* Every man was held to be accountable for the loss of human life because man has been made in the image of God (Genesis 9:5-6). Here, for the first time, the Lord spelled out the sanctity of human life, although the principle had long been in operation as can be seen from His reaction to Abel's murder. However, this is the point at which the dignity of fallen man was spelled out explicitly.

With the new start after the flood, for the first time since the fall, the Lord communicated His will for general living, rather than His will on specific, life-changing events. Mankind was to multiply and fill the earth. All living creatures would have a dread of man and be given into his hands. The implication is that man was expected to act as a responsible steward towards them and manage them appropriately. Here the sanctity of human life was established and man was to be held accountable for taking the life of another.

Although Noah lived for a further 350 years, this is the last recorded occasion when the Lord spoke to him. Once more there was a long period of silence. And once more man degenerated. In Genesis 11 we read of God's intervention in connection with the tower of Babel, scattering mankind over the earth.

So in the opening chapters of Genesis, we find God stepping into the lives of a small number of individuals, seemingly on an *ad hoc* basis, and revealing to them something particular He wanted them to do. The subject-matter of these communications was very specific and it was only after Noah

> God's communication was only to individuals who were at the centre of His purposes and there is no record of His revealing His will to mankind in general or indicating that He had a specific will for every individual.

emerged from the ark that the first instructions for general living were given and recorded. But even these were rather limited in their scope. We need to be careful, of course, not to build a case based on the absence of information but if there were other communications between God and man at that time, these have not been revealed to us.

God's communication was only to individuals who were at the centre of His purposes and there is no record of Him revealing Him will to mankind in general or indicating that He had a specific will for every individual. Even the interactions with Noah were sporadic and people were, up to certain limits, permitted to do what was right in their own eyes.

In Romans 2, Paul discusses the place of the *conscience* in the experience of those who do not possess God's law:

> Indeed, when Gentiles, who do not have the law, do by nature things required by the law, they are a law for themselves, even though they do not have the law, since they show that the requirements of the law are written on their hearts, their consciences also bearing witness, and their thoughts now accusing, now even defending them. (Romans 2:14-15)

It is probable that Paul had in mind his contemporaries, rather than those living, say, in Noah's day. A conscience has to be taught right from wrong and tends to reflect the norms of the society in which the person lives. If moral instruction from God was limited it is hard to see the conscience having a significant impact on the conduct of men at that time.

In fact, there is very little mention of the conscience as such in the Old Testament. In Job 27:6 Job states his determination to keep a clear conscience and in Genesis 20:5 Abimelech, reflecting the norms of his society, protests to God that he has a clear conscience in relation to Sarah because Abraham had told him that she was his sister – a claim that was accepted by the Lord (verse 6).

Thus the Old Testament does not explain the role played by the conscience at that time in relation to the revelation of God's will.

However, with the call of Abram from his home in Ur, a whole new dimension of God's purposes was revealed – the emergence of a special nation – one He wanted to become a kingdom of priests, to minister His truth to the other nations.

Abram to Joseph - God's will for a special nation

In Genesis 12 we read that God instructed Abram to move away from his family.

> The Lord had said to Abram, "Leave your country, your people and your father's household and go to the land I will show you. I will make you into a great nation and I will bless you; I will make your name great, and you will be a blessing. I will bless those who bless you, and whoever curses you I will curse; and all peoples on earth will be blessed through you." (Genesis 12:1-3)

Here we see God's twin promises to Abram – he will be blessed and all nations will be blessed through him. Abram obeyed the Lord and left Ur, and, as he journeyed to the land of Canaan, God periodically stepped into his life, repeating the promises first mentioned in Genesis 12 and supplementing these with other promises:

- the extent of the land that would be given to his offspring (13:14-17);
- the promise of a son and a vast number of descendants, together with the establishment of God's covenant with Abram and a prediction of Israel's oppression and subsequent deliverance (15:1-21);
- God's covenant of circumcision and specific mention of Isaac. Abram and Sarai are also renamed Abraham ("father of many") and Sarah ("princess") (17:1-22);
- the prediction of the timing of the birth of Isaac (18:1-15);

- the promise of Genesis 12 reconfirmed, following Abraham's testing on Mount Moriah (22:15-18).

At each stage God spelled out specific instructions for Abram:

- walk through the land (13:17);
- make a sacrifice (15:9);
- circumcise every male (17:10);
- sacrifice Isaac (22:1-14).

Abraham believed the Lord and obeyed Him at every turn, even to the astonishing length of being willing to sacrifice the child of promise. At other times, too, God interacted directly with Abraham – making arrangements for Ishmael, informing him about the impending destruction of Sodom and Gomorrah, and even offering concessions that resulted in the deliverance of Lot (Genesis 19).

However, there is no apparent moral instruction to Abraham[1]. Abraham believed God and that was credited to him as righteousness (Genesis 15:6) and he obeyed His commands and laws (26:5), but there is little indication of God giving Abraham moral teaching. In fact, when Abraham lied, first to the Egyptians in Genesis 12 and then to Abimelech in Genesis 20, God stepped in to keep His plans on course to preserve Sarah and the line through Isaac.

There is also no evidence of God's interaction with anyone else, apart from Lot, Ishmael and Hagar, all for Abraham's sake (Genesis 19:29; 21:13). The focus is entirely on the line of promise, through Isaac, from whom the nation of Israel was to emerge.

The same process continued with Isaac and Jacob. In Genesis 26, God repeated to Isaac His promises to Abraham while warning him not to go down to Egypt in a time of famine. We are also told that Isaac

---

[1] Genesis 15:2-3 and 16:1-2 indicate that Abram was following a legal system in relation to succession of the family estate. This was probably the Code of Hammurabi or an earlier version of this. Hammurabi was a Babylonian king who, around 1780 BC, created a Code as a legal system covering laws for the lives of citizens and even punishment for criminals.

prospered and became very rich, like his father before him, because God blessed him (25:11; 26:12).

When Jacob encountered the Lord at Bethel, *en route* to Haran (Genesis 28:10-22), God again re-iterated the promise originally given to Abraham with an added assurance that He would guide Jacob in his journey.

> I am with you and will watch over you wherever you go, and I will bring you back to this land. I will not leave you until I have done what I promised you. (Genesis 28:15)

Jacob, like his father, did experience the Lord's blessing and protection. However, the extent of Jacob's acknowledgement of the Lord in his life, prior to his return home, appears somewhat ambiguous: Rachel took the household gods with her when she fled from her father (31:30-34), so worship of the Lord does not appear to be exclusive of other gods. On the other hand, Jacob did recognise the role God had played behind the scenes during his time with Laban:

> If the God of my father, the God of Abraham and the Fear of Isaac, had not been with me, you would surely have sent me away empty-handed. But God has seen my hardship and the toil of my hands, and last night he rebuked you. (Genesis 31:42)

In the latter part of chapter 32, as Jacob neared home, worried about his reception from Esau, we can infer something of his inner turmoil in the account of his literal wrestling with God, but by the time we reach chapter 35, the crisis seems to be over. God told Jacob to go to Bethel (35:1) and build an altar. Jacob by that stage appears to have committed himself fully to the Lord and he ordered the disposal of all "foreign gods" (including, presumably, Rachel's household gods). He also required his company to purify themselves and change their clothes (35:2). At Bethel God again appeared to him and blessed him, renaming him "Israel" and confirming the earlier promises.

I am God Almighty; be fruitful and increase in number. A nation and a community of nations will come from you, and kings will come from your body. The land I gave to Abraham and Isaac I also give to you, and I will give this land to your descendants after you. (Genesis 35: 11-12)

Joseph, Jacob's favoured son, was the next individual on whom the Lord focused His attention. Yet strangely, through all the twists and turns of Joseph's life, there is no record of God's direct communication with him. He was obviously a man of faith and we read that the Lord was with him (e.g. 39:3, 21, 23). Joseph recognised that God had used his brothers' evil act to preserve the entire family.

> Through all the twists and turns of Joseph's life, there is no record of God's direct communication with him.

> God sent me ahead of you to preserve for you a remnant on earth and to save your lives by a great deliverance. (Genesis 45:7)

This is perhaps the first clear example of the truth later expressed by Paul in Romans:

> And we know that in all things God works for the good of those that love him, who have been called according to his purpose. (Romans 8:28)

Although God did not speak directly to Joseph, he was aware that his destiny lay not in Egypt but in Canaan (as his father Jacob reminded him in Genesis 48:21) and as he neared the end of his life Joseph told his brothers of this.

> God will surely come to your aid and take you up out of this land to the land he promised on oath to Abraham, Isaac and Jacob... God will surely come to your aid, and then you must carry my bones up from this place. (Genesis 50:24-25)

Considering the Lord's interactions with mankind up to the end of Genesis, then, we can see the hand of God in the lives of a very few individuals:

- appearing to them on occasion to encourage them;
- speaking to them to give them instructions for particular tasks;
- working behind the scenes to make sure His wider purposes were accomplished.

The methods God used to communicate His will at that time included direct speech, speaking through dreams or, on occasion, through angels. With Abraham, we see the first suggestion of His wider purpose – the establishment of a special nation, through whom God planned to work, and the golden thread of the promises to Abraham ran through the lives of Isaac, Jacob and Joseph.

But it is important to notice that God engaged with only a very few individuals and He engaged with them only on specific matters. He does not seem to have had a plan in mind for every aspect of their lives. He gave precise details to Noah on how to build the ark, but had no comment on his drunken exposure in Genesis 9; He reminded Jacob of His promises to his father, but had nothing to say about his sons' murderous treachery in Genesis 34.

And all the time there was very little moral teaching. Although we see God's judgments on evil in extreme cases (the flood, Babel, and Sodom), a lot of what went on was very dubious, morally. Yet much of it appears without comment and, apparently, without punishment. Genesis sets out God's dealings with the individuals at the heart of His purposes, but we read of no contact with the rest of humanity. His main priority was to get the nation, the people who were to administer His rule on earth, into place.

Exodus opens with the oppression of the Israelites in Egypt and the birth and preservation of Moses. God had already foretold the suffering of the Israelites to Abraham in Genesis 15:13-14 and now in Exodus 2 we read:

God heard their groaning and he remembered his covenant with Abraham, with Isaac and with Jacob. So God looked on the Israelites and was concerned about them. (Exodus 2:24-25)

Moses – the deliverance of the special nation

When God confronted Moses in a burning bush, He commissioned him with the task of delivering Israel from Egypt.

> I am the God of your father, the God of Abraham, the God of Isaac and the God of Jacob ... I have indeed seen the misery of my people in Egypt. I have heard them crying out because of their slave-drivers, and I am concerned about their suffering. So I have come down to rescue them from the hand of the Egyptians and to bring them up out of that land into a good and spacious land, a land flowing with milk and honey... So now, go. I am sending you to Pharaoh to bring my people the Israelites out of Egypt. (Exodus 3:6-10)

In the following chapters of Exodus we read of how the Lord achieved this through Moses and Aaron, giving them eloquence before Pharaoh and signs to back up their words. After the exodus God continued to lead Israel, guiding them by pillars of cloud and fire, delivering them from Pharaoh's army and providing them with manna, quails and water. So, in this way, the Lord began to accomplish His purposes for Israel, leading and feeding them.

However, at the same time He was laying down practices for them to follow in the future: in Exodus 12 we have the institution of the feast of the Passover with the accompanying command that they were to observe this for generations to come (Exodus 12:14); in Exodus 12:48-49 we read that any alien who wanted to celebrate the Passover had to be circumcised; in Exodus 16:29-30 the Sabbath was established as a day of rest.

However, at a more detailed level, Moses had a responsibility to act as a judge among the people, to apply God's will to them on specific issues as he was the one to whom God had revealed His decrees and laws (Exodus 18:15-16). Jethro, Moses' father-in-law, rightly saw that this was an impossible burden and suggested that Moses should delegate some of this work.

> You must be the people's representative before God and bring their disputes to him. Teach them the decrees and laws, and show them the way they are to live and the duties they are to perform. But select capable men from all the people – men who fear God, trustworthy men who hate dishonest gain – and appoint them as officials over thousands, hundreds, fifties and tens. Have them serve as judges for the people at all times, but have them bring every difficult case to you; the simple cases they can decide themselves. (Exodus 18:19-22)

So others were now involved in the application of God's decrees. Moses had to teach the expression of God's will and reliable, God-fearing men were to use their wisdom to apply these decrees to the ordinary situations of life and the disputes that periodically arose between individual Israelites. Here for the first time, we see the beginnings of a God-given way of life. But these men were not given any fresh revelations of God's will in this context: they were to use their wisdom to apply God's previously revealed commands to the situations they found themselves in.

> These men were not given any fresh revelations of God's will in this context: they were to use their wisdom to apply God's previously revealed commands to the situations they found themselves in.

However, when the Israelites arrived at Mount Sinai, God gave them a far greater insight into His plans and purposes for them than ever before, and more details of how they were to live their lives.

> You yourselves have seen what I did to Egypt, and how I carried you on eagles' wings and brought you to myself. Now, if you obey me fully and keep my covenant, then out of all nations you will be my treasured possession. Although the

whole earth is mine, you will be for me a kingdom of priests and a holy nation. (Exodus 19:4-6)

In summary...

God called Abram out of Ur, to lead him to the land of promise, and we can see His hand on Abram and his descendants, Isaac, Jacob and Joseph. He delivered the Israelites from their captivity in Egypt through Moses, who brought the chosen nation to the edge of the land. In God's purposes, the Israelites were to be the ones who were to administer His righteous rule on the earth. As God had promised Abram in Genesis 12, his descendants were not only to be blessed, but to be a means of disseminating God's blessings. The main thrust of God's purposes up to that point was to bring the nation of Israel to the land of promise to fulfil their destiny. As they stood at the foot of Sinai, the Lord was about to reveal His will for them to an extent and in a detail that had never before been experienced by mankind – by the giving of the Ten Commandments and the Law.

Chapter 3
The Law and after

We have seen from Genesis how God spoke, gave dreams or sent angels, to certain leading individuals, to let them know His will for them and, perhaps, their family. The subject matter tended to relate to particular actions the Lord wanted them to take and there is little moral instruction or guidance on general aspects of life.

In the early chapters of Exodus Moses was the man to whom God spoke, guiding and supporting him to bring the Israelites out of Egypt and into the desert. In addition, the Lord revealed to Moses His will for the people on specific issues of morality and conduct. Initially, before Moses had time to write it all down, it was an oral law, and the people came to Moses for every decision. However, this was soon to prove unworkable, as we saw from Exodus 18:13-26. Following Jethro's advice, Moses appointed trustworthy people to apply the laws and decrees given by God. From this we can see how important knowledge and application of God's commandments were to knowing and doing the will of God.

The Ten Commandments and supporting regulations

But when they reached Sinai, the Lord revealed His will to the people of Israel in a much more detailed and systematic way. In Exodus 19 we read how the Lord summoned Moses to the top of Mount Sinai to receive the Ten Commandments and these formed the basis for the expression of His will to Israel. But there was a lot more to the Law than just these commandments. When we look at the detailed laws and requirements contained in Leviticus, Numbers and Deuteronomy we find the expression of God's will for a vast range of aspects of national life. Not all of the instructions were given to Moses on the mountain. The Lord also revealed His will for the Israelites to him in the Tent of Meeting in the desert of Sinai (Numbers 1:1; 9:1), on the plains of Moab by the Jordan (Numbers 36:13) and in the desert area east of

Jordan (Deuteronomy 1:1). We find legal regulations in relation to matters such as:

- Worship
  - Sacrifices; Offerings; Furniture; Vestments
- Ceremonial regulations
  - Dietary rules; Sabbath regulations
- Civil regulations
  - How to treat servants and slaves; How to deal with personal injuries; Protection of property; Social responsibility; Administering of justice in relation to the poor
- Day to day living
  - Medical instructions; Unhealthy sexual practices; Helping your neighbour with lost oxen
- Regulations to manage the land responsibly
  - Mixing crops; Allowing fields to lie fallow
- Warnings against idolatry
- Jubilee celebrations – cancelling debt and freeing slaves

So there was a very wide range of issues for which God revealed His will – everything that was necessary for a God-honouring society of that time. And it is apparent that God was not only interested in the "big issues" – the religious questions. There was no sense of the sacred/secular divide that has characterised Western Christendom. There were regulations to ensure justice, to avoid oppression, to avoid people becoming ultra-rich at the expense of others and to make sure that the poor were looked after.

For example, Exodus 23 laid down detailed regulations for ensuring justice in the law courts:

> Do not deny justice to your poor people in their lawsuits. Have nothing to do with a false charge and do not put an innocent or honest person to death, for I will not acquit the guilty. Do not accept a bribe, for a bribe blinds those who see and twists the words of the righteous. Do not oppress an alien; you yourselves

know how it feels to be aliens, because you were aliens in Egypt. (Exodus 23:6-9)

Particular care was taken to avoid the creation of institutionalised poverty, principally through the Jubilee regulations, whereby, every fiftieth year, all property bought or sold had to be returned to its original owner (see Leviticus 25:8-28).

There were also suggestions that the care and nurture of the land were important. The land was not to be abused and forced. It was to be managed and not bled dry. There had to be responsible use of the land so that it would continue to yield crops in the future.

> For six years you are to sow your fields and harvest the crops, but during the seventh year let the land lie unploughed and unused. Then the poor among your people may get food from it, and the wild animals may eat what they leave. Do the same with your vineyard and your olive grove. (Exodus 23:10-11)

And, interspersed with the individual regulations, there was a repeated warning to obey everything that they were told to do. For example:

> Be careful to do everything I have said to you. Do not invoke the names of other gods; do not let them be heard on your lips. (Exodus 23:13)

> Keep my commands and follow them. I am the Lord. Do not profane my holy name. I must be acknowledged as holy by the Israelites. I am the Lord, who makes you holy and who brought you out of Egypt to be your God. I am the Lord. (Leviticus 22:31-33)

> If you follow my decrees and are careful to obey my commands, I will send you rain in its season, and the ground will yield its crops and the trees of the field their fruit. (Leviticus 26:3-4)

To help Israel to remember, the Lord prescribed tassels on the corners of the Israelites' garments as a reminder of His commands:

> You will have these tassels to look at and so you will remember all the commands of the Lord, that you may obey them and not prostitute yourselves by going after the lusts of your own hearts and eyes. Then you will remember to obey all my commands and will be consecrated to your God. I am the Lord your God, who brought you out of Egypt to be your God. I am the Lord your God. (Numbers 15:39-41)

As Moses neared the end of his life, many of the original instructions given to Israel in Exodus were repeated in more detail in Deuteronomy. Moses preceded this by saying:

> Hear now, O Israel, the decrees and laws I am about to teach you. Follow them so that you may live and may go in and take possession of the land that the Lord, the God of your fathers, is giving you. Do not add to what I command you and do not subtract from it, but keep the commands of the Lord your God that I give you. (Deuteronomy 4:1-2)

The Israelites were more highly privileged than any other nation in that a blueprint for a theocracy (government by divine guidance) was being revealed to them.

> Observe them (the Lord's decrees and laws) carefully, for this will show your wisdom and understanding to the nations, who will hear about all these decrees and say, "Surely this great nation is a wise and understanding people." What other nation is so great as to have their gods near them the way the Lord our God is near us whenever we pray to him? And what other nation is so great as to have such righteous decrees and laws as

this body of laws I am setting before you today? (Deuteronomy 4:6-8)

However, even though the Lord revealed extensive and wide-ranging regulations for Israel, it was not possible to cover every eventuality. Naturally, the people could pray for wisdom to help them make a decision. Alternatively they could go to the priests and judges, who would either decide cases themselves or take them to Moses, and he would consult God. For example, we read in Leviticus 24:10-16 that a person had blasphemed the name of the Lord with a curse. They knew this was wrong, because Exodus 22:28 stated "Do not blaspheme God", but they did not know what to do about it. What should they do with this person? They brought the case to Moses and they put the man "in custody until the will of the Lord should be made clear to them" (Leviticus 24:12).

God revealed to Moses that the punishment was for the entire assembly to stone the man to death (Leviticus 24:13-16). This was then added to the laws and decrees, and became part of the will of God for the people of Israel. There are similar examples in Numbers 9:8-14 (ceremonial uncleanness at the time of Passover) and in Numbers 15:32-36 (gathering wood on the Sabbath day).

So God revealed His will for the people through Moses, in both a systematic and an *ad hoc* way. But Moses was the leader of the people. How did God reveal His will for the everyday life of the ordinary Israelite? Basically, they were to carry out God's commandments, as set out in the Law of Moses. Not everyone could expect to hear the voice of God or receive a message from Him in one way or another. The will of God for the Israelites was to know God's Law and to live according to it.

The expression 'the will of God' is seldom mentioned in the rest of the Old Testament. This is because the will of God for the people of Israel was clearly laid down in the Law of Moses. God wanted

> The expression 'the will of God' is seldom mentioned in the rest of the Old Testament. This is because the will of God for the people of Israel was clearly laid down in the Law of Moses.

them to live in accordance with it. When Moses gave the Law a second time (Deuteronomy) he stated this very clearly.

> If cases come before your courts that are too difficult for you to judge - whether bloodshed, lawsuits or assaults - take them to the place the Lord your God will choose. Go to the priests, who are Levites, and to the judge who is in office at that time. Enquire of them and they will give you the verdict. You must act according to the decisions they give you at the place the Lord will choose. Be careful to do everything they direct you to do. Act according to the law they teach you and the decisions they give you. Do not turn aside from what they tell you, to the right or to the left. (Deuteronomy 17:8-11)

The Law which God gave Moses was extensive and covered practically every aspect of their lives. Provided they followed the Law they were doing the will of God. It was so important to God that His people follow His will, that He guided them by blessing them if they obeyed that Law and judging them if they did not. This is spelt out very clearly in Deuteronomy 28.

> If you fully obey the Lord your God and carefully follow all his commands that I give you today, the Lord your God will set you high above all the nations on earth. All these blessings will come upon you and accompany you if you obey the Lord your God. (Deuteronomy 28:1-2)

Here is the need to fully obey, and verses 3-13 list the blessings that would come upon the nation of Israel if they did obey. They include food, clothing and health (verses 3-6,8,11-12), protection from their enemies (verse 7), and their establishment as a special nation (verses 9-10,13).

Moses finishes this section on blessings with the exhortation:

Do not turn aside from any of the commands I give you today, to the right or to the left, following other gods and serving them. (Deuteronomy 28:14)

This emphasis on agricultural blessing should not surprise us. Many countries today struggle to provide sufficient food for their populations, and in Old Testament (and New Testament) times this was the situation also. To have reliable harvests and good flocks and herds, providing both food and clothing, would go a long way to ensuring they would be a healthy and happy nation.

But what would happen if they disobeyed? The next section of Deuteronomy 28 deals with that.

However, if you do not obey the Lord your God and do not carefully follow all his commands and decrees I am giving you today, all these curses will come upon you and overtake you. (Deuteronomy 28:15)

And if we read the list of curses (judgments) that were to befall the nation of Israel they fall into the same three categories as the blessings. The judgments include no food and clothes (verses 16-18), no protection from enemies (verses 25, 49-50) and loss of status as a special nation (verses 36-37, 43-44).

At the end of Deuteronomy, as Moses was about to die, he summed up the position for the people of Israel as follows:

See, I set before you today life and prosperity, death and destruction. For I command you today to love the Lord your God, to walk in His ways, and to keep his commands, decrees and laws; then you will live and increase, and the Lord your God will bless you in the land you are entering to possess. (Deuteronomy 30:15-16)

This is the justice of the Law of Moses: blessings for obedience, but judgments for disobedience. However, what level of obedience did God require for them to 'fully' obey? It could not have been 100%, for that would imply they needed to be sinless, to obtain these blessings! That being the case, how did Israel know whether or not their compliance was sufficiently high to warrant God's approval? Deuteronomy 28 provides the answer.

> This is the justice of the Law of Moses: blessings for obedience, but judgments for disobedience.

> All these curses will come upon you. They will pursue you and overtake you until you are destroyed, because you did not obey the Lord your God and observe the commands and decrees he gave you. They will be a sign and a wonder to you and your descendants forever. (Deuteronomy 28:45-46)

Thus this system of blessings and judgments was *a sign* to the people of Israel, and as such it guided them. If the nation was being blessed, that was a sign to them that they were meeting God's requirements and following His will. On the other hand if they were suffering, it was a sign to them that they were not, and thus they should repent and turn back to God and His Law.

That generation of Israelites came out of Egypt, wandered in the wilderness and died there. The next generation eventually settled in the Promised Land. In spite of their failures, the Lord fed them with manna and quail, brought water from a rock and their clothes did not wear out (Exodus 16:13,31; 17:6; Numbers 11:31; 20:11; Deuteronomy 8:4). In the land they were protected from their enemies and He did, indeed, bless them under the terms of Deuteronomy 28, even though their obedience was not 100%.They were doing their best to follow the will of God and, by and large, they did well enough to meet with God's approval.

So it was the will of God that all Israelites follow His Law, from the highest to the lowest. In fact the Law of Moses prescribed extra rules for any future king of Israel. For example:

When he takes the throne of his kingdom, he is to write for himself on a scroll a copy of this law, taken from that of the priests, who are Levites. It is to be with him, and he is to read it all the days of his life so that he may learn to revere the Lord his God and follow carefully all the words of this law and these decrees and not consider himself better than his brothers and turn from the law to the right or to the left. Then he and his descendants will reign a long time over his kingdom in Israel. (Deuteronomy 17:18-20)

This shows just how important God considered knowledge of the Law of Moses and obedience to it.

However, the Law of Moses deals mainly with everyday situations which would confront the ordinary person. Sometimes decisions would have to be made, especially by the leaders, which were not moral issues covered by the Law of Moses. These included internal political decisions, or matters involving other nations. Sometimes the Lord spoke to an individual, a judge or king or a prophet, as He did in Genesis or in Exodus with Moses. On other occasions, to obtain God's will on a matter, the political leader had to go to the spiritual leader and enquire (Deuteronomy 17:9-10). They would interpret, or apply, the Law. However, there was another way that God communicated His will to Israelite leaders and that was the curious *Urim* and *Thummim.*

The Urim and Thummim

The Urim and Thummim were possibly two precious stones which Aaron, the High Priest, carried in a pouch over his heart; one signified 'Yes!' and the other 'No!' A question was asked, these stones would be shaken in the pouch and one taken or tossed out, and the answer was taken to be the will of God.

Also put the Urim and the Thummim in the breast-piece, so they may be over Aaron's heart whenever he enters the presence of the Lord. Thus Aaron will always bear the means of making decisions for the Israelites over his heart before the Lord. (Exodus 28:30)

Then Moses brought Aaron and his sons forward and washed them with water. He put the tunic on Aaron, tied the sash around him, clothed him with the robe and put the ephod on him. He also tied the ephod to him by its skillfully woven waistband; so it was fastened on him. He placed the breastpiece on him and put the Urim and Thummim in the breastpiece. (Leviticus 8:6-8)

These may have been used when, in the Old Testament, we read about 'casting lots', used by the people of Israel to find out what to do, for example, where Achan was picked out as the man who had disobeyed the Lord's orders by plundering Jericho (Joshua 7). From the passages in which they occur they appear to have been used to reveal the Lord's will in things of national importance, such as going to war (or not), or finding the Lord's will for the ark of the covenant.

The lot is cast into the lap, but its every decision is from the Lord. (Proverbs 16:33; see also 18:18)[2]

There are very few references to Urim and Thummim and they do not appear to have been used by the ordinary people to work out the Lord's specific will for their lives. In effect, they supplemented the Law in revealing the Lord's will in specific situations of national importance where there was an either/or choice to be made.

In his very old age, Moses learnt that Joshua was to take over from him. Some of the instructions God gave Moses concerning Joshua are found in Numbers 27:18-21. They include Joshua's ability to consult Eleazer the priest to find out the will of God.

---

[2] For more on casting lots and the Urim and Thummim see pp 42-46 of *The Miracles of the Apostles* by Michael Penny, available from The Open Bible Trust (or www.obt.org.uk).

So the Lord said to Moses, "Take Joshua son of Nun, a man in whom is the spirit, and lay your hand on him. Make him stand before Eleazar the priest and the entire assembly and commission him in their presence. Give him some of your authority so that the whole Israelite community will obey him. He is to stand before Eleazar the priest, who will obtain decisions for him by inquiring of the Urim before the Lord. At his command he and the entire community of the Israelites will go out, and at his command they will come in."

On his death-bed Moses pronounced blessings on all the tribes of Israel, including the Levites.

About Levi he said: "Your Thummim and Urim belong to the man you favoured. You tested him at Massah; you contended with him at the waters of Meribah." (Deuteronomy 33:8)

Thus the political leaders of Israel, in matters not covered by the Law, could go to the High Priest and obtain the Lord's decision from the Urim and Thumim, and we can see them doing just that later in the Old Testament.

Prophets

In Exodus 18, we read that Moses, on Jethro's advice, appointed judges to deal with the straightforward problems brought by the people. By the time we reach Numbers 11, complaints against Moses because of the monotony of the people's diet were growing and Moses, in desperation, appealed to the Lord. The Lord's response was to ask him to bring seventy of Israel's elders to the Tent of Meeting:

Then the Lord came down in the cloud and spoke with him, and he took of the Spirit that was on him and put the Spirit on the seventy elders. When the Spirit rested on them, they prophesied, but they did not do so again. (Numbers 11:25)

In the next chapter, Aaron and Miriam rebelled against Moses, claiming that the Lord had also spoken through them, as well as Moses. The Lord then clearly stated the special position held by Moses:

> When a prophet of the Lord is among you, I reveal myself to him in visions, I speak to him in dreams. But this is not true of my servant Moses; he is faithful in all my house. With him I speak face to face, clearly and not in riddles. (Numbers 12:5-8)

Moses, then, was unique in that generation, in that the Lord revealed His will directly to him. Other prophets received the Lord's messages in visions and dreams but these never contradicted what was taught in the

> Moses was unique in that generation, in that the Lord revealed His will directly to him.

Law. In Deuteronomy, there are instructions on how to identify false prophets – if they encourage the worshipping of other gods (13:1-3) or if their predictions do not come true (18:20-22).

But Moses was nearing the end of his life. How would the Lord communicate His will after Moses was gone? Moses explained to the people in Deuteronomy 18:

> The Lord said to me... I will raise up for them a prophet like you from among their brothers; I will put my words in his mouth, and he will tell them everything I command him. (18:17-18)

Although the statement is rightly applied to Christ in the New Testament (Acts 3:22; 7:37) it seems also to have had an immediate application to Moses' immediate successor, and, in the opening chapter of Joshua, we find the Lord fulfilling His promise made through Moses and speaking directly with Joshua.

In summary...

The people of Israel were at a critical stage in their history and required detailed guidance. So God regularly came down in a cloud to the Tent of Meeting and spoke directly with Moses, revealing His instructions for the people. He also communicated His will to prophets, through dreams and visions, but this appears to be a rather infrequent occurrence.

Occasionally, in relation to certain, very specific, one-off situations, the political leaders could consult the High Priest who would use Urim and Thummim to obtain a decision, and God would communicate His will through these.

However, the most important way in which God expressed His will was by the Law given to Moses. The Law of Moses *was* the will of God for all the people of Israel. It was what God wanted the people of Israel to do, from the lowest to the highest, and it dealt in detail with every aspect of their lives. There were extra demands on the priests and future kings and those extras were also contained within the Law. It was clear; it was specific; it was written down. The application of the Law to specific daily problems was administered by Moses and wise priests and judges who knew the Law. If the people 'fully' obeyed the Law, they would be blessed; if they disobeyed they would be judged (Deuteronomy 28). And if the leaders *did not* follow the Law, then they should not expect decisions or guidance from any other means, whether in dreams or from the Urim and Thummim.

Although the Law catered for all aspects of the life of the Israelites, there seems to be no suggestion that God had a particular "purpose" for the life of every individual, other than the requirement to live a holy and moral life by observing the Law. His individual will for Moses, as leader of the people, was set out clearly and in detail, but this does not appear to be the case for the ordinary people. Furthermore, in Moses' instructions to the Israelites, there is no suggestion that they should seek God's "particular will" for themselves, on issues such as where they should live or who they should marry. Their responsibility was to obey the Law. This was the key to blessing.

Chapter 4
The historical books of the Old Testament:
Joshua to Nehemiah

The cycle of idolatry

After the death of Moses, Joshua was given the task of leading the people into the promised land and, in the opening chapter of the book of Joshua, the Lord spoke directly to him, encouraging him, promising him success and assuring him of His presence. But the key to that success lay in his obedience to the Law of Moses.

> Be strong and very courageous. Be careful to obey all the law my servant Moses gave you; do not turn from it to the right or to the left, that you may be successful wherever you go. Do not let this Book of the Law depart from your mouth; meditate on it day and night, so that you may be careful to do everything written in it. Then you will be prosperous and successful. (Joshua 1:7-8)

As indicated in the previous chapter, the Lord's will for the people of Israel was contained in the Law and Joshua was faithful in implementing the Lord's instruction. In Joshua 5 we find the re-establishment of circumcision and the keeping of the Passover. When Joshua built an altar to the Lord, we read that he built it "according to what was written in the Book of the Law of Moses" (Joshua 8:31). As Joshua neared the end of his life he left instructions for the people which echoed the words the Lord had given him long before as he prepared to enter the land:

> The Lord's will for the people of Israel was contained in the Law and Joshua was faithful in implementing the Lord's instruction.

> Be very strong; be careful to obey all that is written in the Book of the Law of Moses, without turning aside to the right or to the left. Do not associate with these nations that remain among you; do not invoke the names of their gods or swear by them... If you violate the covenant of the Lord your God, which he commanded you, and go and serve other gods and bow down to them, the Lord's anger will burn against you and you will quickly perish from the good land he has given you. (Joshua 23:6-7, 16)

This was a prophetic warning and at the start of the book of Judges we read that:

> The people served the Lord throughout the lifetime of Joshua and of the elders who outlived him and who had seen all the great things the Lord had done for Israel... After that whole generation had been gathered to their fathers, another generation grew up, who knew neither the Lord nor what he had done for Israel. Then the Israelites did evil in the eyes of the Lord and served the Baals. (Judges 2:7, 10-11)

Thereafter, the history of Israel throughout the books of Judges, Samuel, Kings and Chronicles is a sad litany of a cycle of:

- Israel and her kings doing evil in the eyes of the Lord by serving other gods (e.g. Judges 10:6; 2 Kings 13:11);
- The Lord punishing Israel, usually by allowing their enemies to defeat them (e.g. Judges 10:7; 2 Kings 13:3);
- The Israelites crying out to the Lord, who raised up a judge or a new king who delivered the people and re-instituted worship of the Lord and obedience to the Law (e.g. Judges 10:10-11:33; 2 Kings 10:30). Sometimes, as in the case of Jehu in 2 Kings 10, the return to the Lord was only partial, with worship of the Canaanite gods still practised in Israel and Judah. (The 12 tribes of Israel split into two following civil war after Solomon's reign. Ten tribes formed

the northern kingdom, Israel, and two formed the southern kingdom, Judah.)

There are echoes here of the Lord's warning to the nation in Deuteronomy 28 that obedience to the Law would result in blessing, but disobedience would bring judgment. Throughout the historical books we see repeated iterations of that process.

The Lord's revelation of His will on specific issues

In this period the Lord communicated His will on *specific* matters not covered by the Law by three means:

- *Speaking directly to the leaders of the people*: God spoke directly to Joshua (e.g. Joshua 8), David (2 Samuel 2:1) and Solomon (1 Kings 3:5). However, this appears to be on rare occasions, far less frequently than during the time before the Law was given;
- *Speaking to prophets who communicated His will to the leaders and the people*: There are many instances of this throughout the historical books (e.g. 1 Samuel 3:19-21; 2 Samuel 12:1-12; 1 Kings 21:17-29; 2 Kings 3:11-12, 16; 2 Chronicles 11:2-4);
- *The use of lots, such as Urim and Thummim*. This appears to have been very rare. Joshua used lots to identify Achan as the one who had disobeyed his orders in relation to the spoils from Jericho (Joshua 7). Urim and Thummim are mentioned in 1 Samuel 28:6 and Ezra 2:63 (repeated in Nehemiah 7:65) but there is no record of their use.

During this time, the most frequent form of direct communication from the Lord came through the mouths of prophets, who encouraged kings to follow the Lord or condemned them for not doing so (e.g. 1 Samuel 7:2-6; 1 Kings 14:7-11; 2 Kings 1:16-17; 2 Chronicles 24:19-22).

In the historical books and the prophetic writings there are some 27 instances of, or references to, a practice of "inquiring of God."

This is mostly done through prophets – e.g. 1 Kings 22:5-8, 2 Kings 8:8, Jeremiah 37:7. 1 Samuel 9:9 explains that:

> Formerly in Israel, if a man went to inquire of God, he would say, "Come, let us go to the seer," because the prophet of today used to be called a seer.

The inquiries were usually done by kings, judges or other leaders (21 cases) and the most common inquiry was whether they would be given success in war (10 cases - e.g. 1 Samuel 23:2,4, 1 Kings 22:5-8, Jeremiah 21:2). However, there are single instances of a wide variety of subjects including the reasons for a famine (2 Samuel 21:1), whether a king will recover from an illness (2 Kings 8:8) and even how lost donkeys could be found (1 Samuel 9:6). It does appear that ordinary people could 'enquire of God,' a phrase used in Exodus 18:15 (*KJV*) to describe Moses' practice of resolving everyday disputes among the people.

Throughout the historic books, there are periodic references to the Law of Moses and the need to follow it. During Israel's most blessed period, the reigns of David and Solomon, the Law of Moses was emphasised. 1 Chronicles 16 tells us that David left Zadok the priest at Gibeon to present burnt offerings to the Lord "in accordance with everything written in the Law of the Lord" (1 Chronicles 16:39-40). David's final words to Solomon stressed the importance of following the Law:

> "... be strong, show yourself a man, and observe what the Lord your God requires: Walk in his ways, and keep his decrees and commands, his laws and requirements, as written in the Law of Moses, so that you may prosper in all you do and wherever you go, and that the Lord may keep his promise to me: 'If your descendants watch how they live, and if they walk faithfully before me with all their heart and soul, you will never fail to have a man on the throne of Israel.'" (1 Kings 2:2-4)

When the Lord appeared to Solomon in 1 Kings 3, offering to give him anything he asked, Solomon, realising that he could not rely on God's direct advice for all problems, prayed for wisdom to govern the people. So again, as with

When the Lord appeared to Solomon in 1 Kings 3, offering to give him anything he asked, Solomon, realising that he could not rely on God's direct advice for all problems, prayed for wisdom to govern the people.

the representatives appointed by Moses, we see that the Lord expected wise men to apply the Law to specific situations and to deal justly with the people. When Solomon completed the temple, he delivered a prayer of dedication of the building to the Lord, thanking Him for all His goodness to Israel and asking Him to fulfil His promises to the nation in spite of their failings. The Lord subsequently appeared to Solomon and confirmed that He had heard his prayer.

> As for you, if you walk before me as David your father did, and do all I command, and observe my decrees and laws, I will establish your royal throne, as I covenanted with David your father ... (2 Chronicles 7:17-18)

Unfortunately, Solomon's obedience to the Lord was incomplete and he angered the Lord by following other gods (1 Kings 11:9). After the division of the kingdom during the reign of Solomon's son Rehoboam we find a succession of kings who either followed the Lord (and were victorious) or worshipped Canaanite gods (and were defeated) and the Law of Moses appears to have slipped from the centre of the nation's life and at times it was even lost.

2 Kings 17:13-15 sums up the position:

> The Lord warned Israel and Judah through all his prophets and seers: "Turn from your evil ways. Observe my commands and decrees, in accordance with the entire Law that I commanded your fathers to obey and that I delivered to you through my servants the prophets." But they would not listen and were as stiff-necked as their fathers, who did not trust in the Lord their

God. They rejected his decrees and the covenant he had made with their fathers and the warnings he had given them. They followed worthless idols and themselves became worthless.

Good kings and bad

From time to time individual kings would discover the Law and re-introduce its observance. Asa, king of Judah, encouraged by Azariah the prophet, "commanded Judah to seek the Lord, the God of their fathers, and to obey his laws and commands" (2 Chronicles 14:4). He also removed the symbols of Baal worship from the land. His son, Jehoshaphat, also sought the Lord in his early years:

> In the third year of his reign he sent his officials...to teach in the towns of Judah... They taught throughout Judah, taking with them the Book of the Law of the Lord; they went round to all the towns of Judah and taught the people. (2 Chronicles 17:7-9)

Josiah, king of Judah, who was a worshipper of the Lord, found the Book of the Law in the temple and was appalled at what he read there because he recognised the extent of the nation's failure.

> Go and inquire of the Lord for me and for the remnant in Israel and Judah about what is written in this book that has been found. Great is the Lord's anger that is poured out on us because our fathers have not kept the word of the Lord; they have not acted in accordance with all that is written in this book. (2 Chronicles 34:21; see also 2 Kings 22:8,11-13)

The response of Huldah the prophetess was uncompromising:

> This is what the Lord says: "I am going to bring disaster on this place and its people – all the curses written in the book that has been read in the presence of the king of Judah. Because they have forsaken me and burned incense to other gods and

provoked me to anger by all that their hands have made, my anger will be poured out on this place and will not be quenched." (2 Chronicles 34:24-25)

Josiah removed the idols and re-introduced the celebration of Passover and, because he humbled himself before the Lord, the judgment on the nation did not take place during his lifetime (2 Chronicles 34:27-28).

However, kings loyal to the Law were few and far between and by the end of 2 Chronicles both Israel and Judah were in exile because of their idolatry and failure to follow the Law (Deuteronomy 28:45,49-50,64).

> Kings loyal to the Law were few and far between and by the end of 2 Chronicles both Israel and Judah were in exile because of their idolatry and failure to follow the

Exile and restoration

The reasons for the exile of both Israel and Judah are clearly stated:

> This (the deportation of Israel to Assyria) happened because they had not obeyed the Lord their God, but had violated his covenant – all that Moses the servant of the Lord commanded. They neither listened to the commands nor carried them out. (2 Kings 18:12)

> … they (the people of Judah) mocked God's messengers, despised his words and scoffed at his prophets until the wrath of the Lord was aroused against his people and there was no remedy. He brought up against them the king of the Babylonians, who killed their young men with the sword in the sanctuary, and spared neither young man nor young woman, old man or aged. God handed them all over to Nebuchadnezzar. (2 Chronicles 36:16-17)

God had revealed His will for the people in the Law, re-enforced through the words of the prophets and occasionally by direct communication to the leaders. The people were expected to follow the instructions of their rulers. However, since the kings of Israel and Judah, by and large, persisted in idolatry, either alongside or instead of worship of the Lord, the people followed suit.

The only way ordinary individuals could obtain specific instruction from God on issues not covered by the Law was by 'inquiring' of Him, almost invariably through prophets or priests. There is no suggestion that God communicated any specific instruction as to His will directly to ordinary individuals, nor is there any suggestion that the ordinary people should seek such communication: their primary duty was to follow the Law of the Lord, administered by their leaders.

Nevertheless, although the kings of Israel and Judah turned their backs on the Lord and followed the practices of the nations around them, He did not forget His covenant relationship with the nation and He pitied them. For example:

> ... the Lord was gracious to them (Israel) and had compassion and showed concern for them because of his covenant with Abraham, Isaac and Jacob. To this day he has been unwilling to destroy them or banish them from his presence. (2 Kings 13:23)

While the people were punished for their idolatry, they were not completely destroyed and the Lord worked behind the scenes to accomplish His wider purposes. Jeremiah predicted that Judah would serve the king of Babylon for seventy years, after which Babylon would be punished for its evil (Jeremiah 25:11-12). 2 Chronicles closes with the announcement of the restoration of Judah as the Lord moved the heart of Cyrus, who had conquered Babylon, to bring about the restoration of Jerusalem.

> In the first year of Cyrus king of Persia, in order to fulfil the word of the Lord spoken by Jeremiah, the Lord moved the heart of Cyrus king of Persia to make a proclamation throughout his realm and to put it in writing: "This is what Cyrus king of Persia says: 'The Lord, the God of heaven, has given me all the

kingdoms of the earth and he has appointed me to build a temple for him at Jerusalem in Judah. Anyone of his people among you – may the Lord his God be with him, and let him go up.'" (2 Chronicles 36:22-23)

Nehemiah had recognised that the motivation for his actions was put into his heart by the Lord (Nehemiah 2:12). Now here He influenced the mind of a Gentile king to fulfil His plans. The books of Ezra and Nehemiah record how these plans were accomplished. He was not the only Gentile ruler to be moved by the Lord in this way. Ezra[3] indicates that Artaxerxes was also influenced by the Lord in bringing honour to the house of the Lord in Jerusalem (Ezra 7:27-28).

However, when Ezra and Nehemiah rebuilt Jerusalem and the people who were moved by God to go back (Ezra 1:5) had returned from exile, it is important to see the central role that the Law of Moses played in the restored nation. When the people settled in their towns, the morning and evening sacrifices were re-introduced "in accordance with what is written in the Law of Moses" (Ezra 2:3); the Feast of Tabernacles, and other appointed feasts were celebrated "in accordance with what is written" (Ezra 3:4); when the temple was completed the priests and Levites were installed "according to what is written in the Book of Moses"

> When Ezra and Nehemiah rebuilt Jerusalem, and the people returned from exile, it is important to see the central role that the Law of Moses played in the restored nation.

(Ezra 6:18); Passover was celebrated. (Ezra 6:19-22). Ezra was at the heart of these developments because:

> Ezra had devoted himself to the study and observation of the Law of the Lord, and to teaching its decrees and laws in Israel. (Ezra 7:10)

Even Artaxerxes confirmed Ezra's responsibilities:

---

[3] In fact Ezra 6:14 indicates that there were three Persian kings involved in instructing the building of the temple.

> And you, Ezra, in accordance with the wisdom of your God, which you possess, appoint magistrates and judges to administer justice to all the people of Trans-Euphrates – all who know the laws of your God. And you are to teach any who do not know them. Whoever does not obey the law of your God and the law of the king must surely be punished by death, banishment, confiscation of property, or imprisonment (Ezra 7:25-26)

So here we can see the re-introduction of the earlier model – the use of wise men like Ezra, who had an understanding of the Law of the Lord to administer the Law, both in the religious and the day to day lives of the people. In the book of Nehemiah we also read of the work Ezra was doing.

> ... on the first day of the seventh month, Ezra the priest brought the Law before the assembly, which was made up of men and women and all who were able to understand. He read it aloud from daybreak till noon as he faced the square before the Water Gate in the presence of men, women and others who could understand. And all the people listened attentively to the Book of the Law. (Nehemiah 8:2-3)

Nehemiah 8 also records in more detail the celebration of the Feast of Tabernacles, mentioned in Ezra 3, and in Nehemiah 9 and 10 we read of Israel's confession of their sins and a re-commitment of themselves to the Lord and His covenant.

> The rest of the people...all who separated themselves from the neighbouring peoples for the sake of the Law of God ... now bind themselves with a curse and an oath to follow the Law of God given through Moses the servant of God and to obey carefully all the commands, regulations and decrees of the Lord our God. (Nehemiah 10:28-29)

In summary...

When Israel entered the land under Joshua's leadership, guided by the Law of Moses, the outlook had looked so promising. Sadly, they disobeyed the Law and corrupted themselves by worshipping the idols of the surrounding nations. The period of time leading up to exile for both houses of Israel was characterised by a turning away from God followed by a partial repentance, which invariably proved to be short-lived. During this time the Law of Moses, the primary expression of God's will for the people, became obscured from their view. Eventually they were conquered by the Babylonians and taken into captivity. Towards the end of that seventy year exile the Lord, through Cyrus and Nehemiah, brought about the rebuilding of Jerusalem and its temple. They were aided by Ezra, the priest, whose task it was to restore the religious life of the returning exiles by re-establishing the Law at the heart of national life.

So, by the end of the book of Nehemiah, the people were back in the land, to some extent chastened by their exile experiences, and the Law of Moses again became the primary expression of the Lord's will for the nation. The will of God for individuals was expressed through the Law, interpreted and applied by wise men. Direct communication between God and even the leaders of the nation appeared to have ceased and there is no suggestion that God spoke directly to individual Israelites on life-decisions or on matters of conduct. He had expressed His will in the Law and there was nothing to be added to it.

After the temple was rebuilt, there was a period of some four hundred years of silence from God. Malachi is the only prophet who spoke during this time and he is generally believed to have done so fairly soon after Ezra and Nehemiah. The picture he paints is one of a diminishing number of godly people in Israel and of a nation who have largely turned away from God and whose worship had declined to a formality, with abuses and widespread corruption.

This section has considered the historical books of the Old Testament. During this period other Old Testament books were written – the 'Wisdom literature' and the prophets. The next two sections will consider the light that these books shed on the way in which God revealed His will.

Chapter 5
The wisdom writings and poetry

The Old Testament contains several books of poetry and wisdom. The authors of these books – Job, Psalms, Proverbs, Ecclesiastes and Song of Songs – write as individuals trying to follow the will of God and, because of the nature of the writing, the material is largely personal. They therefore give us insight into the characteristics of the man or woman of God and explore the experiences, temptations and frustrations that affect our lives in a fallen world.

Fear of the Lord

Job is generally believed to be the earliest book in the Old Testament and was certainly written before the Law was given. God declared that there was no one like him and he is introduced to us as one who is:

> … blameless and upright: he feared God and shunned evil. (Job 1:1)

"Fearing" the Lord does not mean to be frightened of Him; it means to revere and respect Him and to be in awe of Him. The emphasis on "fearing" God and shunning evil is repeated in Job 28:28:

> The fear of the Lord - that is wisdom, and to shun evil is understanding.

There we see a first reference to "wisdom", which is developed in more detail in Proverbs.

When Job pleads his case before God in Job 29:11-17, he lists his own merits, which reveals some of the qualities that characterise the life of someone who is "blameless and upright." They include:

- helping the poor
- being righteous
- showing justice
- championing the cause of the disadvantaged people in society.

> There is consistency between the ideas expressed in this early literature and the instructions spelled out for the nation of Israel through the Law of Moses.

All of these characteristics are also considered in greater detail in Proverbs and the requirement for Israel to follow them is stated in the Law of Moses – e.g. Exodus 23:1-9. There is thus a consistency between the ideas expressed in this early literature and the instructions spelled out for the nation of Israel through the Law of Moses.

As far as the dating of the other wisdom and poetry books is concerned, all the writers of the Psalms lived after the Law was given, with almost half (seventy three) being attributed to David. Proverbs, Ecclesiastes and Song of Songs were largely written by Solomon, although Proverbs 30 and 31 may have been composed by earlier writers.

Ecclesiastes, like Job, speaks of the fear of the Lord as an important part of the duty of man:

> I know that it will go better with God-fearing men, who are reverent before God. Yet because the wicked do not fear God, it will not go well with them, and their days will not lengthen like a shadow. (Ecclesiastes 8:12-13)

At the end of the book, as Solomon pulls together all the strands of the philosophical arguments he has debated, he concludes:

> Now all has been heard; here is the conclusion of the matter: Fear God and keep his commandments, for this is the whole duty of man. (Ecclesiastes 12:13)

This effectively sums up the requirements for the people of Israel to follow the will of the Lord, and the book of Proverbs also majors on the theme of the fear of God. The key word in Proverbs is "wisdom" and at the start of the book we read that:

> The fear of the Lord is the beginning of knowledge, but fools despise wisdom and discipline. (Proverbs 1:7)

What is wisdom? It is not head knowledge or intellectual prowess. It is the ability to live appropriately. It has connotations of discretion, prudence, understanding, the ability to exercise judgment and self-discipline. In other words, it is knowledge in action. And it begins with the fear of the Lord – a reverence for Him, recognising His exclusive right to Lordship over us and all aspects of our lives. It involves an acknowledgement of His relationship to us as Lord and a structuring of our values in the light of that acknowledgement. There are a number of things said in Proverbs about the fear of the Lord:

- Those who seek wisdom understand the fear of the Lord. (Proverbs 2:5)
- To fear the Lord is to hate and avoid evil. (Proverbs 8:13)
- To fear the Lord brings hope for the future. (Proverbs 23:17-18)
- Fearing the Lord leads to blessing. (Proverbs 28:14)

"Fear of the Lord" appears in Proverbs as a prerequisite for following the Lord's will for life. There is one passage in Proverbs that really sums up the idea behind this:

> "Fear of the Lord" appears in Proverbs as a prerequisite for following the Lord's will for life.

> Trust in the Lord with all your heart and lean not on your own understanding; in all your ways acknowledge him, and he will make your paths straight. Do not be wise in your own eyes; fear the Lord and shun evil. This will bring health to your body and nourishment to your bones. (Proverbs 3:5-8)

To Solomon this was central to finding the Lord's will - trusting in Him, fearing Him and obeying His commands. Here also the description of Job (Job 1:1), is picked up by Solomon. Unfortunately, Solomon, for all his wisdom, was unable to follow his own advice consistently.

Social justice

Much of Proverbs is written in the form of advice from a father to a son and, although many of the issues discussed are relevant to any young person growing up (e.g. the dangers of adultery, excessive drinking or mixing with bad company), it is clear that the "son" is someone who was expected to play a responsible role in society. Advice is given on requirements for a just society - from the point of view of a king, or others who are in positions of influence, dealing with issues such as:

Concern for the poor

This is dealt with on three levels:

- At a personal level: whoever is kind to the poor lends to the Lord (Proverbs 19:17), while whoever mocks the poor shows contempt for his Maker (Proverbs 17:5);
- At the level of someone in a position of power: those who exploit the poor and crush the needy in court will find that the Lord will take up their case (Proverbs 22:22-23);
- At the level of someone in authority who is able to do something about poverty: the Lord requires him to speak up for the destitute, who cannot speak for themselves (Proverbs 31:8).

So God here expected the people to have a personal concern for the poor. A person in a powerful position should not abuse them (e.g. by taking them to court) but must also stand up for and protect the poor in a society where they are being oppressed. In fact, Proverbs identifies God with the poor to the extent that Proverbs 14:31 says:

He who oppresses the poor shows contempt for their Maker, but whoever is kind to the needy honours God.

Concern for justice more generally

In Proverbs justice is praised; when justice is done, it brings joy to the righteous (Proverbs 21:15); by justice a king gives a country stability (Proverbs 29:4); if a ruler judges the poor with fairness, his throne will always be secure (Proverbs 29:14).

Concern for right behaviour in business

Proverbs also warns against corrupt practices in commercial life: the businessman is urged to be generous and to pay debts when they are due (Proverbs 3:27-28); there are repeated warnings against the use of dishonest scales (e.g. Proverbs 11:1) and accepting bribes (e.g. Proverbs 17:23).

These are by no means exhaustive, but they indicate the types of issues on which the Lord expressed His will for His people, Israel. This was how He expected them to behave if they were to be a righteous nation. These ideas expressed in Proverbs back up the instructions given to the people through the Law. For example:

There will always be poor people in the land. Therefore I command you to be open-handed towards your brothers and towards the poor and needy in your land. (Deuteronomy 15:11)

Do not pervert justice; do not show partiality to the poor or favouritism to the great, but judge your neighbour fairly. (Leviticus 19:15)

Do not use dishonest standards when measuring length, weight or quantity. Use honest scales and honest weights, an honest ephah and an honest hin. (Leviticus 19:35-36)

Personal characteristics that please or displease the Lord

Proverbs also sets out the personal characteristics that the Lord hates and that the Lord takes delight in. Evil characteristics recur throughout Proverbs. There are frequent negative references to pride and haughtiness, lying, violence, deception for gain, evil, bearing false witness and stirring up dissention in family and other close groups. These are summed up in Proverbs 6:16-19:

> There are six things the Lord hates, seven that are detestable to him: haughty eyes, a lying tongue, hands that shed innocent blood, a heart that devises wicked schemes, feet that are quick to rush into evil, a false witness who pours out lies and a man who stirs up dissention among brothers.

There are also a lot of characteristics that the Lord takes delight in: the promotion of peace, generosity, kindness to the needy, rewarding evil with good, diligence, and telling the truth. For example:

> The Lord detests lying lips, but he delights in men who are truthful. (Proverbs 12:22)

> A generous man will himself be blessed, for he shares his food with the poor. (Proverbs 22:9)

> If your enemy is hungry, give him food to eat; if he is thirsty, give him water to drink. In doing this, you will heap burning coals on his head, and the Lord will reward you. (Proverbs 25:21, 22)

When we turn to the Psalms we find these positive and negative personal characteristics originally set out in the Law repeated. The Psalmists advocate uprightness in heart, justice, truth, having clean hands rather than indulging in lies, deceit, violence, flattery, slander, bribery. To the Psalmists, the key to walking with God is a righteous life. For example:

> Lord, who may dwell in your sanctuary? ... He whose walk is blameless and who does what is righteous, who speaks the truth from his heart ... who does his neighbour no wrong and casts no slur on his fellow-man, who ... honours those who fear the Lord, who keeps his oath even when it hurts, who ... does not accept a bribe against the innocent. He who does these things will never be shaken. (Psalm 15:1-5)

The Psalms also echo the themes of justice that we find in Proverbs:

> God presides in the great assembly; he gives judgment among the "gods": "How long will you defend the unjust and show partiality to the wicked? Defend the cause of the weak and fatherless; maintain the rights of the poor and oppressed. Rescue the weak and needy; deliver them from the hand of the wicked." (Psalm 82:1-4)

> Righteousness and justice are the foundation of your throne; love and faithfulness go before you. (Psalm 89:14)

The Law of the Lord

In these passages we can see the lifestyle principles laid down for Israelites in the Law being echoed by the national poets. However, in the Psalms there is a more explicit emphasis on following the Law of the Lord. Psalm 1 sets the scene. The man who is blessed does not associate with the wicked. Instead:

> ... his delight is in the law of the Lord, and on his law he meditates day and night. He is like a tree planted by streams of water, which yields its fruit in season and whose leaf does not wither. Whatever he does prospers. (Psalm 1:2-3)

What a wonderful picture of stability and strength! Sustained by the Law of the Lord he makes a success of every aspect of his life. In fact the overwhelming message of the Psalms is that the Lord wants His people to trust Him and follow His Law. Example after example is given of the benefits and vindication that come from putting one's trust in the Lord and in loving His Word. For example:

> As for God, his way is perfect; the word of the Lord is flawless. He is a shield for all who take refuge in him. (Psalm 18:30)

> Example after example is given of the benefits and vindication that come from putting one's trust in the Lord and in loving His Word.

> The law of the Lord is perfect, reviving the soul. The statutes of the Lord are trustworthy, making wise the simple. The precepts of the Lord are right, giving joy to the heart. The commands of the Lord are radiant, giving light to the eyes. The fear of the Lord is pure, enduring forever. The ordinances of the Lord are sure and altogether righteous ... By them is your servant warned; in keeping them there is great reward. (Psalm 19:7-11)

> The mouth of the righteous man utters wisdom, and his tongue speaks what is just. The law of his God is in his heart; his feet do not slip. (Psalm 37:30-31)

> I desire to do your will, O my God; your law is within my heart. (Psalm 40:8)

> May your unfailing love come to me, O Lord, your salvation according to your promise; then I will answer the one who taunts me, for I trust in your word. (Psalm 119:41-42)

Psalm 119 is a remarkable Psalm in that almost every one of its 176 verses contains a reference to God's word in one form or another.

In summary...

The primary will of God for the nation of Israel was that they should fear Him and keep His commandments, as Solomon stated in Ecclesiastes 12:13. The commandments were set out in the Law of Moses and its supporting regulations. Fearing God involved offering Him exclusive worship and was the key to wise living. The wisdom books illustrate in poetic language how the principles for godly conduct in the Law worked themselves out in daily life. In the literature, we can see that many of these ideas are interconnected. So for Israel at that time, fearing the Lord involved:

- living righteously and shunning evil behaviour, which is evidence of true wisdom;
- helping the underprivileged and using personal influence to create a just society;
- trusting the Lord and His Word and committing our way to Him and
- experiencing the blessings that come on those who live wisely.

Fear of the Lord included offering Him exclusive worship. The historic books of the Old Testament catalogue Israel's failure to do this consistently, and the punishments which resulted. During this time, the Lord raised up prophets to communicate His will to the people and the next section considers their message.

Chapter 6
The prophets

The historical books of the Old Testament record the role played by a number of prophets in revealing the Lord's will to the people of Israel and Judah, encouraging the national leaders to follow the Lord and warning them of the consequences of disobeying the Mosaic Law. The prophets also gave specific advice to leaders from time to time on matters such as whether or not to go to war. However, their words were largely ignored and the position is summed up in 2 Chronicles 36:15-16:

> The Lord, the God of their fathers, sent word to them through his messengers again and again, because he had pity on his people and on his dwelling place. But they mocked God's messengers, despised his words and scoffed at his prophets until the wrath of the Lord was aroused against his people and there was no remedy.

However, the Old Testament contains the writings of 16 prophets, composed over a period of some 320 years, from the reigns of kings Uzziah of Judah and Jeroboam of Israel around 690 BC[4] to the period after the nation was restored to the land, around 370 BC. These prophecies expand on the information given in the historical books about the work of the prophets and provide a fuller picture of their message. Three prophets (Jonah, Amos and Hosea), wrote to Israel, while the others wrote to Judah, although there is overlap (e.g. Amos and Hosea both contain warnings to Judah).

The three failures of the nation

The prophets condemned the nation for three failures to follow the will of God:

---

[4] The dates used in this book are taken from *The Companion Bible*

1. Rejecting the Lord and following other gods

As we have noted in the historic books, Israel had a fatal attraction to the gods of the nations around them. The prophets repeatedly warned them of the consequences of idolatry. For example:

> "I will punish her for the days she burned incense to the Baals; she decked herself with rings and jewellery, and went after her lovers, but me she forgot," declares the Lord. (Hosea 2:13)

> I will pronounce my judgments on my people because of their wickedness in forsaking me, in burning incense to other gods and in worshipping what their hands have made. (Jeremiah 1:16)

It is not possible to understate the seriousness of this sin. The relationship between the Lord and Israel is compared in the Scriptures to that of a marriage, so worshipping idols was tantamount to adultery and even prostitution. Old Testament prophets repeatedly used this metaphor. For example, Jeremiah used the picture of a marriage to express the Lord's anger at His rejection by both Israel and Judah.

> ... the Lord said to me, "Have you seen what faithless Israel has done? She has gone up on every high hill and under every spreading tree and has committed adultery there ... I gave faithless Israel her certificate of divorce and sent her away because of all her adulteries. Yet I saw that her unfaithful sister Judah had no fear; she also went out and committed adultery. Because Israel's immorality mattered so little to her, she defiled the land and committed adultery with stone and wood." (Jeremiah 3:6, 8-9)

The relationship between the Lord and Israel is compared to that of a marriage, so worshipping idols was tantamount to adultery and even prostitution.

2. Neglecting the law

In the first of the Ten Commandments, the Lord warned Israel that they were to have no other gods before Him (Exodus 20:3), so Israel's first sin was in breaking that commandment. However, the prophets also condemned the nation for neglecting the Law of Moses more generally.

> ... as tongues of fire lick up straw and as dry grass sinks down in the flames, so their roots will decay and their flowers blow away like dust; for they have rejected the law of the Lord Almighty and spurned the word of the Holy One of Israel. (Isaiah 5:24)

> Why has the land been ruined and laid waste ... ? The Lord said, "It is because they have forsaken my law, which I set before them; they have not obeyed me or followed my law." (Jeremiah 9:12-13)

The Law of Moses was the fundamental expression of God's will for Israel but, as the historical books indicate, the nation's idolatry led to an abandonment of the Law. Even at times when the Lord's regulations were being followed, the people's religious observances were corrupted and their lifestyles so inconsistent with the Lord's standards that He would not accept their sacrifices.

> Stop bringing meaningless offerings! Your incense is detestable to me. New Moons, Sabbaths and convocations – I cannot bear your evil assemblies...When you spread out your hands in prayer, I will hide my eyes from you...Your hands are full of blood; wash and make yourselves clean. Take your evil deeds out of my sight! Stop doing wrong, learn to do right! Seek justice, encourage the oppressed. (Isaiah 1:13, 15-17)

Here Isaiah also put his finger on the third failure of the nation – permitting injustice in their society.

3. *Failing to practise justice*

The historical books record the Lord's provision through the Law of Moses for a just society in Israel – one that would be a source of admiration to the nations around (Deuteronomy 4:6-8), but they failed to practise justice. As we saw earlier, the Psalmists and the writers of Proverbs spoke out against this and the prophets also condemned injustice in the nation:

> "Take your evil deeds out of my sight! Stop doing wrong, learn to do right! Seek justice, encourage the oppressed. Defend the cause of the fatherless, plead the case of the widow." (Isaiah 1:16-17)

> This is what the Lord says: "For three sins of Israel, even for four, I will not turn back my wrath. They sell the righteous for silver, and the needy for a pair of sandals. They trample on the heads of the poor as upon the dust of the ground and deny justice to the oppressed." (Amos 2:6-7)

> Woe to those who plan iniquity, to those who plot evil on their beds! At morning's light they carry it out because it is in their power to do it. They covet fields and seize them, and houses and take them. They defraud a man of his home, a fellowman of his inheritance. Therefore, the Lord says, I am planning disaster against this people. (Micah 2:1-3)

> Israel and Judah would not listen and both kingdoms became corrupted by idolatry, injustice and their rejection of the Lord and His Law.

Exile and restoration

A major aspect of the prophet's role was to act as the conscience of the nation, speaking into specific situations to encourage, warn or correct the people. Unfortunately, Israel and Judah would not listen and both kingdoms became corrupted by idolatry, injustice and their rejection of the Lord and His Law. For each of these sins the wrath of God was directed against the people and the prophets warned that ultimately the land would be destroyed and the people taken into exile.

> "You have lifted up the shrine of your king, the pedestal of your idols, the star of your god – which you made for yourselves. Therefore I will send you into exile beyond Damascus," says the Lord, whose name is God Almighty. (Amos 5:26,27)

> "I will hand all Judah over to the king of Babylon, who will carry them away to Babylon or put them to the sword." (Jeremiah 20:4)

These warnings were no idle threats; Israel was taken off into exile by the Assyrians about 611 BC (2 Kings 18:11) and Judah by the Babylonians around 477 BC (2 Kings 25:21).

However, the message of the prophets was not completely bleak. As we have seen, the prophets picture Israel as the Lord's wife. Hosea was instructed to marry an adulterous woman to depict the relationship between the Lord and His people. After she had been unfaithful to him, the Lord spoke to him again:

> The Lord said to me, "Go, show your love to your wife again, though she is loved by another and is an adulteress. Love her as the Lord loves the Israelites, though they turn to other gods and love the sacred raisin cakes." (Hosea 3:1)

The Lord still loved His covenant people and remembered the promises He had made to the patriarchs. So His rejection of them was not to be permanent. Several prophets predicted the return of both houses of Israel to the land after captivity.

To Israel Amos wrote:

> In that day I will restore David's fallen tent. I will repair its broken places, restore its ruins, and build it as it used to be... I

will bring back my exiled people Israel; they will rebuild the ruined cities and live in them... I will plant Israel in their own land, never again to be uprooted from the land I have given them," says the Lord your God. (Amos 9:11, 14-15)

Zephaniah, while warning Judah of approaching destruction, saw beyond the exile to a time when the fortunes of Jerusalem would be restored.

> Sing, O Daughter of Zion; shout aloud, O Israel! Be glad and rejoice with all your heart, O daughter of Jerusalem! The Lord has taken away your punishment, he has turned back your enemy. The Lord, the king of Israel, is with you; never again will you fear any harm. (Zephaniah 3:14-15)

Jeremiah was more specific and predicted that Judah's exile in Babylon would last for 70 years:

> This is what the Lord says: "When seventy years are completed for Babylon, I will come to you and fulfil my gracious promise to bring you back to this place." (Jeremiah 29:10)

As the end of the 70 year period approached, Daniel, exiled in Babylon, pleaded with the Lord to remember His promise, spoken through Jeremiah (Daniel 9:2, 3) and confessed the faults of his people. Daniel's confession effectively summed up the way the Lord had revealed His will to the nation and their condemnation for failing to follow that revelation.

> We have not obeyed the Lord our God or kept the laws he gave us through his servants the prophets. All Israel has transgressed your law and turned away, refusing to obey you. Therefore the curses and sworn judgments written in the Law of Moses, the servant of God, have been poured out on us, because we have sinned against you. (Daniel 9:10-11)

The Law of God had been given through Moses, arguably the greatest prophet the nation had seen. It laid down regulations for the religious, commercial and social lives of the people and was the fundamental way in which the Lord revealed His will for the nation. Successive prophets were raised up when Israel turned away and they called the people to return to the Lord and His Law and to practise justice in society, as the Law prescribed. Both Israel and Judah failed to do this and were punished by the Lord: the land was laid waste and the people were taken into exile.

But the Lord's ultimate purposes were not to be thwarted and He remembered His covenant with His people. Israel would be restored to the land and the nations who had oppressed them would be punished, as several prophets testify. Ezekiel, for example, in chapters 25-32, sets out the Lord's judgment against several nations for their treatment of His people. Isaiah foresaw the Lord's judgment on Assyria and Babylon, the instruments of God's punishment on Israel and Judah.

"O my people who live in Zion, do not be afraid of the Assyrians, who beat you with a rod and lift up a club against you, as Egypt did. Very soon my anger against you will end and my wrath will be directed to their destruction." (Isaiah 10:24-25)

> Israel would be restored to the land and the nations who had oppressed them would be punished, as several prophets testify.

"Sit in silence, go into darkness, Daughter of the Babylonians; no more will you be called queen of kingdoms. I was angry with my people and desecrated my inheritance; I gave them into your hand...Now, then, listen, you wanton creature, lounging in your security and saying to yourself, 'I am, and there is none besides me. I will never be a widow or suffer the loss of children.' Both of these will overtake you in a moment, on a single day ..." (Isaiah 47:5-6, 8-9)

The everlasting covenant to come

However, several of the prophets, in addition to their concerns with contemporary issues, had seen visions of a future day when God would establish His king on David's throne and set up a kingdom that would permanently unite the two houses of Israel under a new covenant. Ezekiel, among others, foresaw this day:

> This is what the Sovereign Lord says... "I will make them one nation in the land, on the mountains of Israel. There will be one king over all of them and they will never again be two nations or be divided into two kingdoms... My servant David will be king over them, and they will all have one shepherd. They will follow my laws and be careful to keep my decrees... I will make a covenant of peace with them; it will be an everlasting covenant." (Ezekiel 37:21-22, 24, 26)

Jeremiah also spoke of this "everlasting covenant."

> "In those days, at that time," declares the Lord, "the people of Israel and the people of Judah together will go in tears to seek the Lord their God... They will come and bind themselves to the Lord in an everlasting covenant that will not be forgotten." (Jeremiah 50:4-5)

One of the features of the new covenant would be complete obedience to the Law of the Lord. Jeremiah explained the nature of the new covenant:

> "The time is coming," declares the Lord, "when I will make a new covenant with the house of Israel and with the house of Judah. It will not be like the covenant I made with their forefathers... because they broke my covenant, though I was a husband to them," declares the Lord. "This is the covenant that I will make with the house of Israel after that time," declares

the Lord. "I will put my law in their minds and write it on their hearts. I will be their God and they will be my people." (Jeremiah 31:31-33)

Again we can see the importance of the Law as the expression of God's will for His people. His kingdom rule from Jerusalem will be characterised by perfect obedience to His Law, which will be "written on the hearts" of His people.

Ezekiel said that David would be king at that time, and this idea also occurs in Jeremiah 30:9 and Hosea 3:5. It is debatable whether God really meant that David himself would be raised or whether the king would be one of his descendants, but Isaiah predicted the coming of a child who would take His place on David's throne. The words are very familiar to us:

> His kingdom rule from Jerusalem will be characterised by perfect obedience to His Law, which will be "written on the hearts" of His people.

For to us a child is born, to us a son is given, and the government will be on his shoulders. And he will be called Wonderful Counsellor, Mighty God, Everlasting Father, Prince of Peace. Of the increase of his government and peace there will be no end. He will reign on David's throne and over his kingdom, establishing and upholding it with justice and righteousness from that time on and forever. (Isaiah 9:6-7)

The first part of this prophecy was fulfilled some 600 years after it was spoken by Isaiah, when God broke into human experience in a completely new and wonderful way – by sending the Lord Jesus to the nation. He came at an inauspicious time, with Israel under Roman occupation. The Lord Jesus Christ, as the Word made flesh (John 1:14), revealed the Lord and His will for men in an altogether more intimate way.

In summary...

The function of the prophets was to prompt the people as to the will of God for their time. They did this by encouraging the people to be faithful to the Lord and His Law, warning and, where necessary, threatening them with the consequences of their idolatry, disobedience and sinful behaviour. The prophets also revealed the will of God for specific situations and advised the national leaders on what action they should take. Jeremiah, for example, repeatedly advised Judah's King Zedekiah that the kingdom would be taken by Nebuchadnezzar and that he should surrender to him.

Although the message of the prophets was grim in places, with exile as the punishment for both houses of Israel, there was also a message of hope. Israel would one day be restored, with the rightful king, from David's line, reigning over a united nation. At that time the Law of the Lord would be perfectly obeyed by Israel because it would be written on their hearts.

Chapter 7
The will of God in
the Old Testament:
Summary and Conclusion

From the Garden of Eden to Abraham, the Scriptures give us snapshots of God's dealings with specific individuals, advising them of what He wanted them to do, either by direct instruction, through angels or by dreams. With the call of Abraham, we find something more systematic, as the Lord revealed His purpose of blessing the world through Abraham's descendants – a purpose repeated to successive generations up to the time of Joseph.

The opening chapters of Exodus find the Israelites released from oppression in Egypt and Moses administering God's will for the people's life in their 40 year journey through the wilderness. Moses was in a special relationship with God and He spoke to him face to face, rather than in dreams or visions, which was the method of revelation to other prophets (Numbers 12:5-8). However, Moses was not physically able to deal in detail with every situation that called for discernment of God's will. As a result he appointed a number of wise, God-fearing men who could apply the principles revealed by the Lord to specific circumstances (Exodus 18:15-22).

With the coming of the Law at Sinai, and following that, we find a much clearer and more detailed expression of God's will for citizens of the Israelite nation. The Ten Commandments and supporting requirements described in the Pentateuch reveal the mind of God for the people of Israel. This is particularly brought home to us by the Lord's

> The Ten Commandments and supporting requirements described in the Pentateuch reveal the mind of God for the people of Israel. This is particularly brought home to us by the Lord's statement in Deuteronomy 4:6-8 that, if His laws were consistently applied, Israel would be the envy of the world.

statement in Deuteronomy 4:6-8 that, if His laws were consistently applied, Israel would be the envy of the world:

> "Observe them carefully, for this will show your wisdom and understanding to the nations, who will hear about all these decrees and say, 'Surely this great nation is a wise and understanding people.'... What other nation is so great as to have such righteous decrees and laws as this body of laws I am setting before you today?" (Deuteronomy 4:6-8)

The Pentateuch systematically sets out the regulations in codified form but further commentary on them, and their application, is provided by the philosophers of Job, Proverbs, and Ecclesiastes and the poets and songwriters in the Psalms and Song of Songs. In addition, the prophets reminded the people of the Lord's will and provided authoritative guidance on how the principles of the Mosaic Law were to be applied to the daily life of the nation.

The historical books of the Old Testament indicate that there were four principal ways in which God communicated His will to the Israelites:

- through direct speech to the leaders – kings or priests;
- through the mouths of prophets;
- through the use of lots (which seems to have been very rare);
- through the Law of Moses and supporting regulations.

This last way was the most significant method the Lord used to express His will. The other three methods tended to be for leaders to deal with the application of the Law to particular situations not explicitly covered by the Law.

So how can we sum up the will of God as expressed through the Mosaic Law?

The first requirement was to worship the Lord only. The Lord is a jealous God and the Ten Commandments open with a reminder of what He had done for Israel and a warning that they should have no other gods before Him (Exodus 20:3). Failure to follow this commandment was a recurring complaint against Israel, as the historical books and the prophets describe, and resulted in their exile from the land.

Secondly, there was a body of religious observances. Regulations were laid down for matters such as worship, sacrifices, festivals, circumcision, Sabbath observance and dealing with 'clean' and 'unclean' animals and objects. However, although these were very explicit legal rules, the prophets repeatedly pointed out that they were expected to keep the 'spirit' of the Law rather than just the letter. For example:

> "Stop bringing meaningless offerings! Your incense is detestable to me. New Moons, Sabbaths and convocations – I cannot bear your evil assemblies... When you spread out your hands in prayer I will hide my eyes from you... Your hands are full of blood... Stop doing wrong and learn to do right! Seek justice, encourage the oppressed." (Isaiah 1:13,15-17)

> Circumcise your hearts, therefore, and do not be stiff-necked any longer. (Deuteronomy 10:16)

The legal requirements were not just to be carefully followed; they were to be accompanied by a lifestyle that was consistent with the societal and personal aspects of the Law. There was no merit in people following religious observances if their conduct was inappropriate and they had failed to love their neighbour.

Thirdly, there were the civic aspects of the Law. There were detailed requirements to ensure justice in the structure of Israel's society. The Law laid down regulations to ensure that there was justice in society, that vulnerable members such as widows, orphans and aliens were not oppressed. The Jubilee and related regulations were designed to prevent poverty from becoming institutionalised in society. The regulations were laid down in the Law but it was the prophets and philosophers who constantly reminded the people to put these principles into practice. The book of Proverbs emphasizes the importance of care for the poor on a national as well as a personal level. The prophets also repeatedly condemned the nation for their failure to practise justice in society.

Finally, there was the personal dimension to the Law. God's vision for the type of individuals He wanted His people to be was set out in the Law. However, the detailed practice was addressed in the wisdom books, the poetry and the prophetic writings. They were to live in the wisdom that comes from the fear of the Lord and shows itself in shunning evil and living righteously, helping vulnerable people and using influence to create a just society.

> The Lord demanded a just society where people loved their neighbours and did not oppress them. That, ultimately, was the full expression of the Law.

Although the will of God was expressed through a legal code, it is important to realise that following that will was not a matter of wooden compliance with regulations. The rituals spoke of something greater – physical circumcision represented a trusting in God rather than self. However, unless it was accompanied by 'circumcision of the heart' it meant little. The Lord demanded a just society where people loved their neighbours and did not oppress them. That, ultimately, was the full expression of the Law.

However, many of the religious practices of Israel – the sacrifices, the Passover Lamb – pointed to the One who was to come – the Lord Jesus Christ, the Lamb of God who was to take away the sin of the world. The next section of the book examines the will of God for His people at the time of the Lord's earthly ministry and beyond.

Section 2

God's revelation of His will

in the New Testament

Chapter 8
The will of God in the Gospels

The four Gospels tell us about a new situation. The Christ (Messiah) promised to the Jewish people in the Old Testament had now arrived. This One, Jesus of Nazareth, was the Son of God, and spoke with the authority of God. He came to Israel and the nation was asked to recognise Him as their Messiah. Putting their trust in Him was the way to eternal life:

> Just as Moses lifted up the snake in the desert, so the Son of Man must be lifted up, that everyone who believes in him may have eternal life. (John 3:14-15)

But what was the place of the law after the Lord's coming? The world was going to be different, but was the will of God for His people going to be different?

We have seen that the will of God for Israel in the Old Testament was primarily to live their lives in accordance with the Law of Moses, not just dutifully and reluctantly but willingly and sincerely. Does this change when we come to the New Testament? Were they still expected to keep that Mosaic Law?

After His baptism the Lord Jesus was led into the wilderness and there He was tempted by the Devil for forty days. However, He overcame the Devil not with the power of His deity, but with three quotations from the Law of Moses. In each case, the Messiah rebuffed the temptation by quoting the Law, demonstrating its continuing importance. The following comes from Matthew 4:3-10.

> The tempter came to him and said, "If you are the Son of God, tell these stones to become bread." Jesus answered, "It is written: 'Man does not live on bread alone, but on every word that comes from the mouth of God.'" [A quotation from Deuteronomy 8:3.]

Then the devil took him to the holy city and had him stand on the highest point of the temple. "If you are the Son of God," he said, "throw yourself down. For it is written: "'He will command his angels concerning you, and they will lift you up in their hands, so that you will not strike your foot against a stone.'" Jesus answered him, "It is also written: 'Do not put the Lord your God to the test.'" [A quotation from Deuteronomy 6:16.]

Again, the devil took him to a very high mountain and showed him all the kingdoms of the world and their splendour. "All this I will give you," he said, "if you will bow down and worship me." Jesus said to him, "Away from me, Satan! For it is written: 'Worship the Lord your God, and serve him only.'" [A quotation from Deuteronomy 6:13.]

Here Christ gave strong affirmation to the Law of Moses. He showed its importance and use, and how it should be adhered to. But His words were even stronger when He started His ministry.

"Do not think that I have come to abolish the Law or the Prophets; I have not come to abolish them but to fulfil them. I tell you the truth, until heaven and earth disappear, not the smallest letter, not the least stroke of a pen, will by any means disappear from the Law until everything is accomplished. Anyone who breaks one of the least of these commandments and teaches others to do the same will be called least in the kingdom of heaven, but whoever practises and teaches these commands will be called great in the kingdom of heaven." (Matthew 5:17-19)

The Gospels continue on from the Old Testament. The main group of people in the Gospels is the same group that dominates the Old Testament, the people of Israel.

This should not surprise us because the Gospels continue on from the Old Testament. The main group of people in the Gospels is the same group that dominates the Old Testament, the people of Israel.

So here, at the start of our Lord's ministry, we see complete endorsement of the Law of Moses. Some Christians find this perplexing, thinking the Gospels must be different from the Old Testament, but let us think about the Lord and His work.

Jesus Christ's sacrifice was for the sins of the world, both Jews and Gentiles. His life was an example to everyone, both Jews and Gentiles. However, it was He who said, "I was sent only to the lost sheep of Israel" (Matthew 15:24) and we read that Christ was "a servant (minister, *KJV*) of the Jews" (Romans 15:8). Thus His ministry, while He was on earth, was to the Jews, a people who were under the Law of Moses and, as such, the will of God for them, at that time, was the same as it had been for their forefathers: to obey the Law of Moses and to be the people God wanted them to be, with the right attitude, namely one of love towards God and their neighbour.

> One of them, an expert in the law, tested him with this question: "Teacher, which is the greatest commandment in the Law?" Jesus replied: "'Love the Lord your God with all your heart and with all your soul and with all your mind.' This is the first and greatest commandment. And the second is like it: 'Love your neighbour as yourself.' All the Law and the Prophets hang on these two commandments." (Matthew 22:35-40)

Here Christ highlighted these two love commandments, but He also endorsed other commandments from the Law when He spoke to the rich ruler in Luke 18:20 and the rich young man in Matthew 19:16-19.

> Now a man came up to Jesus and asked, "Teacher, what good thing must I do to get eternal life?" "Why do you ask me about what is good?" Jesus replied. "There is only One who is good. If you want to enter life, obey the commandments." "Which ones?" the man inquired. Jesus replied, "'Do not murder, do not commit adultery, do not steal, do not give false testimony,

honour your father and mother,' and 'love your neighbour as yourself.'" (Matthew 19:16-19)

The rich young man had kept all these commandments, but the Lord put His finger on the one stumbling-block in his life – his wealth. Only by giving up his wealth could he follow the Lord, but he was not willing to do this. He had kept all the commandments relating to his outward conduct, but he failed to have no other gods before the Lord.

In John 7, the Lord again brings together God's will and obedience to the Law.

> Not until halfway through the Feast did Jesus go up to the temple courts and begin to teach. The Jews were amazed and asked, "How did this man get such learning without having studied?" Jesus answered, "My teaching is not my own. It comes from him who sent me. If anyone chooses to do *God's will*, he will find out whether my teaching comes from God or whether I speak on my own. He who speaks on his own does so to gain honour for himself, but he who works for the honour of the one who sent him is a man of truth; there is nothing false about him. *Has not Moses given you the law? Yet not one of you keeps the law.* Why are you trying to kill me?" (John 7:14-19)

It has been argued by some theologians that the Law was abolished when Christ came. This argument is based on the fact that the Lord was constantly opposing the teaching of the Pharisees, who held themselves out as the great upholders of the Law. However, what He was opposing were their *additions* to the Law of Moses.

The Pharisees and the Law of Moses

Because of Christ's battles with the Pharisees some believe that Christ was dismantling the Law of Moses. Consider, for example, the following:

At that time Jesus went through the cornfields on the Sabbath. His disciples were hungry and began to pick some ears of corn and eat them. When the Pharisees saw this, they said to him, "Look! Your disciples are doing what is unlawful on the Sabbath." (Matthew 12:1-2)

To harvest crops on the Sabbath day was against the Law of Moses, but picking food to eat was not. For example, the first day of the Feast of Tabernacles was a Sabbath, but they could pick fruit from trees (Leviticus 23:35, 40). Also the Law permitted them to pick grapes and grain from their neighbour's field to eat there and then, but they could not harvest them. That would be stealing.

If you enter your neighbour's vineyard, you may eat all the grapes you want, but do not put any in your basket. If you enter your neighbour's cornfield, you may pick the ears with your hands, but you must not put a sickle to his standing corn. (Deuteronomy 23:24-25)

This restriction on picking food to eat on the Sabbath is one example of the Pharisaic additions to the Law of Moses, and Christ opposed these. Others included fasting twice a week, whereas the Law of Moses stipulated one day a year, on the Day of Atonement (Luke 18:12 and Leviticus 23:27). The Law of Moses specified giving a tenth of certain things, whereas the Pharisees stated that people should give a tenth of everything, even minute amounts of herbs and spices (Matthew 23:23; Luke 18:12).

We read of many of these Pharisaic additions to the Law in Mark 7, where they are referred to as "the traditions of the elders" (Mark 7:3, 5). They taught that eating with unwashed hands from unwashed dishes made a person 'unclean' (Mark 7:1-4), but this was not in the Law of Moses and Christ exposed that view as totally wrong teaching (Mark 7:20-23).

There was another very serious Pharisaic addition that Christ condemned in no uncertain terms:

"For Moses said, 'Honour your father and your mother,' and, 'Anyone who curses his father or mother must be put to death.' But you say that if a man says to his father or mother: 'Whatever help you might otherwise have received from me is Corban' (that is, a gift devoted to God), then you no longer let him do anything for his father or mother. Thus you nullify the word of God by your tradition that you have handed down. And you do many things like that." (Mark 7:10-13)

Thus Christ opposed the extra regulations the Pharisees added to the Law of Moses. He did not oppose that Law. However, the Lord Jesus Christ did, Himself, extend that Law, by applying it, not just externally, to actions and speech, but internally, to hearts and minds.

> Christ opposed the extra regulations the Pharisees added to the Law of Moses. He did not oppose that Law. However, the Lord Jesus Christ did extend that Law, by applying it to hearts and minds.

Grace and truth came through Jesus Christ

There is a verse in John's Gospel which, some suggest, shows that the Law was done away with when Christ came. There we read:

> For the law was given through Moses; grace and truth came through Jesus Christ. (John 1:17)

We need to be careful how we understand this verse for clearly, above, we see our Lord's support for the Law of Moses.

'Grace and truth' may be a figure of speech, hendiadys. This is when two words are used, but only one thing is meant. We talk about 'bread and butter' but mean just one - 'buttered bread'. Thus 'grace and truth' may be best understood as 'true grace'. The fact is that there was grace in the Old Testament, in general, and in the Law in particular. We read, for example:

Abraham believed the Lord, and He credited it him as righteousness. (Genesis 15:6; quoted by Paul in Romans 4:3)

The righteous shall live by his faith. (Habakkuk 2:4; quoted by Paul in Romans 1:17)

'Faith' is the basis for righteousness, which is freely given to those who believe. People are 'saved by grace through faith' and we read of 'grace' in such places as:

He mocks proud mockers but gives grace to the humble. (Proverbs 3:34)

Though grace is shown to the wicked, they do not learn righteousness. (Isaiah 26:10)

Then, again, in the Old Testament there are nearly forty references to God being gracious. For example:

The Lord, the Lord, the compassionate and gracious God, slow to anger, abounding in love and faithfulness, maintaining love to thousands, and forgiving wickedness, rebellion and sin. (Exodus 34:6-7)

The Lord bless you and keep you; the Lord make his face shine upon you and be gracious to you; the Lord turn his face toward you and give you peace. (Numbers 6:24-26)

There was also the sacrifice of animals for the atonement of sin; thus the people of that time were not judged then and there for their sins. However, Hebrews 10:4 was careful to point out that "it is impossible for the blood of bulls and goats to take away sins." Although the sacrifices were not effectual in

> Although the sacrifices were not effectual in forgiving sins, God, in His grace, accepted them in anticipation of the one, effective sacrifice that was to come.

forgiving sins, God, in His grace, accepted them in anticipation of the one, effective sacrifice that was to come. Those sacrifices were pictures, or types, of the one true sacrificial Lamb: the Lord Jesus Christ. He was "the Lamb of God, who takes away the sin of the world!" (John 1:29).

The Law was given through Moses, but that Law did demonstrate grace. However, true grace (grace and truth), real grace, came through Jesus Christ. He was the fulfilment. As Paul puts it in one of his later letters:

> These are a shadow of the things that were to come; the reality, however, is found in Christ. (Colossians 2:17)

An extended Law

In the Old Testament, the Lord set out His will for the people of Israel through the Law, which governed every aspect of their behaviour. However, in the Gospels, for example in the Sermon on the Mount, the Lord Jesus applied the commandments, not just to their external behaviour, but to their hearts, minds and motivations.

Compare the following statements taken from Matthew 5:21-48.

Matthew 5:21 You have heard that it was said to the people long ago, 'Do not murder, and anyone who murders will be subject to judgment.'	Matthew 5:22 But I tell you that anyone who is angry with his brother will be subject to judgment.
Matthew 5:27 You have heard that it was said, 'Do not commit adultery.'	Matthew 5:28 But I tell you that anyone who looks at a woman lustfully has already committed adultery with her in his heart.
Matthew 5:31 It has been said, 'Anyone who divorces his wife must give her a certificate of divorce.'	Mathew 5:32 But I tell you that anyone who divorces his wife, except for marital unfaithfulness, causes her to become an adulteress.
Matthew 5:33 Again, you have heard that it was said to the people long ago, 'Do not break your oath, but keep the oaths you have made to the Lord.'	Matthew 5:34-35 But I tell you, Do not swear at all: either by heaven, for it is God's throne; or by the earth, for it is his footstool; or by Jerusalem, for it is the city of the Great King.
Matthew 5:38 You have heard that it was said, 'Eye for eye, and tooth for tooth.'	Matthew 5:39 But I tell you, Do not resist an evil person. If someone strikes you on the right cheek, turn to him the other also.
Matthew 5:43 You have heard that it was said, 'Love your neighbour and hate your enemy.'	Matthew 5:44-45 But I tell you: Love your enemies and pray for those who persecute you, that you may be sons of your Father in heaven.

Here we see the Lord Jesus taking the commandments in the Law of Moses, which dealt with external actions and words, and applying them internally to the hearts and minds. He wanted His followers to be loving and forgiving. Earlier we read that when asked which was the greatest commandment in the Law, the Lord gave not one command, but two: to love the Lord your God with all your heart and with all your soul and with all your mind and to love your neighbour as yourself (Matthew 22:35-40). However, we can see in Matthew 5:44 that He extended this to loving your enemies.

He also gave His followers a very specific new commandment:

> "A new command I give you: Love one another. As I have loved you, so you must love one another. By this everyone will know that you are my disciples, if you love one another." (John 13:34-35).

And the Saviour emphasised to the twelve the importance of His followers loving one another a little later.

> "My command is this: Love each other as I have loved you ... This is my command: Love each other." (John 15:12, 17)

It was important for those Jewish Christians not only to follow the Law of Moses but also to follow what Christ commanded. So much so that we read:

> "If you love me, you will obey what I command." (John 14:15)

> "Whoever has my commands and obeys them, he is the one who loves me." (John 14:21)

> "If you obey my commands, you will remain in my love." (John 15:10)

> "You are my friends if you do what I command." (John 15:14)

So Christ took the actions and words prescribed in the Law of Moses, and applied them to hearts and minds. As such these passages go beyond the Law. Here the Lord was saying that to be His disciples they should not only obey the Law of Moses, they should also obey His commands. This is more than just keeping the Law, it is following it in the way it was meant to be kept; i.e. from the heart. This is similar to what the prophets and the wisdom writers in the Old Testament encouraged. Christ wanted a love and obedience to God that went beyond the Law. He wanted a self-sacrificing love that was like the love He had for us – the love that lays down its life.

> Christ wanted a love and obedience to God that went beyond the Law. He wanted a self-sacrificing love that was like the love He had for us – the love that lays down its life.

The Father's Will

> "For I have come down from heaven not to do my will but to do the will of him who sent me. And this is the will of him who sent me, that I shall lose none of all that he has given me, but raise them up at the last day. For my Father's will is that everyone who looks to the Son and believes in him shall have eternal life, and I will raise him up at the last day." (John 6:38-40)

In this passage we find another aspect of God's will. Everyone who believes in His Son will have eternal life. Thus the will of God for those living when Christ was on earth was not only to follow the Law of Moses and Christ's commandments, it was also to believe in Jesus; that He was the Christ, the Messiah, the Son of God. This, in fact, was the reason why John wrote his gospel.

> Jesus did many other miraculous signs in the presence of his disciples, which are not recorded in this book. But these are written that you may believe that Jesus is the Christ, the Son of God, and that by believing you may have life in his name. (John 20:30-31)

The prophets testified to Israel what miraculous signs the Messiah would do when He came to save them. For example, in Isaiah 35:4-6 we read of four very specific ones:

> "Be strong, do not fear; your God will come … he will come to save you." Then will the eyes of the blind be opened and the ears of the deaf unstopped. Then will the lame leap like a deer, and the mute tongue shout for joy.

Christ performed these miraculous signs and more, and He appealed to those miracles when challenged by the Jews.

> The Jews gathered round him, saying, "How long will you keep us in suspense? If you are the Christ, tell us plainly." Jesus answered, "I did tell you, but you do not believe. The miracles I do in my Father's name speak for me … even though you do not believe me, believe the miracles, that you may know and understand that the Father is in me, and I in the Father." (John 10:24-25, 38)

In Luke 7 we have the account of John the Baptist sending his disciples to the Lord to ask Him, "Are you the one who was to come, or should we expect someone else?" (Luke 7:19-20). Interestingly the Lord did not answer directly but said:

> "Go back and report to John what you have seen and heard: the blind receive sight, the lame walk, those who have leprosy are cured, the deaf hear, the dead are raised, and the good news is preached to the poor." (Luke 7:22; compare Isaiah 35:4-5)

Here, He pointed to the miracles as His credentials. Sadly, however, in spite of all the miraculous signs the Lord did in the presence of the Jewish leadership, we read "they still would not believe in him" (John 12:37).

In Summary...

Jesus was a great defender of the Law of Moses. What He opposed was the Pharisaic additions to that Law. For Him, and for His people the Jews, who were alive during the Gospel period, doing the will of God consisted in following the Law of Moses, not in a wooden, literal sense, but in the spirit in which it was intended, showing the same, self-sacrificing love that the Lord demonstrated to His disciples.

It also included believing that Jesus was the Son of God, the Christ, Israel's Messiah. He was the Lamb of God who took away the sin of the world and He was the means of forgiveness of sins and the way to eternal life.

> For God so loved the world that he gave his one and only Son, that whoever believes in him shall not perish but have eternal life. (John 3:16)

At the start of His ministry we saw a resounding endorsement of the Mosaic Law (Matthew 5:17-19; and note also 4:1-10), and after His resurrection, when addressing His disciples, we have another:

> He said to them, "This is what I told you while I was still with you: Everything must be fulfilled that is written about me in the Law of Moses, the Prophets and the Psalms." Then he opened their minds so they could understand the Scriptures. (Luke 24:44-45)

This would equip them for the challenges that lay ahead. However, they would not be on their own. Earlier He had given them a very specific and significant promise.

> And I will ask the Father, and he will give you another Counsellor to be with you forever – the Spirit of truth. The

world cannot accept him, because it neither sees him nor knows him. But you know him, for he lives with you and will be in you ... But the Counsellor, the Holy Spirit, whom the Father will send in my name, will teach you all things and will remind you of everything I have said to you." (John 14:16-17, 26)

The will of God in the Gospels is very much linked with keeping the Law of Moses, but extends the Old Testament regulations to cover the spirit as well as the letter of the Law. The Lord Jesus was the fulfiller of the Law – the one true sacrifice for sins, to whom the Old Testament pictures pointed. He was also the fulfiller of Israel's expectations – the Messiah who had been promised to the nation in the Old Testament. Therefore, following the will of God also included belief in Jesus as the sacrifice for sin, the Son of God and the Messiah (the Christ).

However, times were changing: God's salvation had a much wider focus than simply the people of Israel, and the early Jewish Christians were about to be taught by that Counsellor who was to be given to them on the day of Pentecost. They were to learn that there were further dimensions to God's will that were still to be revealed.

Chapter 9
The will of God
during the Acts Period

The majority of the New Testament letters were written during the period of time covered by the book of Acts. As such we have many documents to call upon. Not only is there the Acts of the Apostles, but we have fourteen letters. Most of these were written specifically to Jewish Christians: Hebrews, James, 1 & 2 Peter, 1 & 2 & 3 John, Jude and Revelation. This may seem surprising, but in Galatians 2:9 we read that James, Peter and John agreed that they would concentrate on the Jews and, as we can see from their letters, and from what is recorded of them in the Acts of the Apostles, this was exactly what they did.

During this time, Paul also wrote several letters: Galatians, 1 & 2 Thessalonians, 1 & 2 Corinthians and Romans. These were addressed to particular churches, but these churches had a mixture of Jewish and Gentile members. Some parts of these letters deal with issues pertaining to Jewish Christians, some to Gentile Christians, and some to both groups. This is what makes them, in places, hard to understand.

However, up to the first part of the Acts of the Apostles, the Bible has been concerned principally with the people of Israel. We have seen that the will of God for these people was primarily obedience to the Law of Moses. That being the case, we shall consider first the *Jewish* Christians of the Acts Period. What was God's will for them? Was the Mosaic Law still important?

Two common misconceptions

There are two common misconceptions in this context. They are that the Lord finished with the people of Israel when they crucified Christ and that, from the cross onwards, there was no need to

> There are two common misconceptions in this context. They are that the Lord finished with the people of Israel when they crucified Christ and that, from the cross onwards, there was no need to follow the Law.

follow the Law.

An honest reading of the Acts of the Apostles will easily prove this wrong. Acts starts with the day of Pentecost when "there were staying in Jerusalem God-fearing Jews from every nation under heaven" (Acts 2:5). We read that about 3,000 of them accepted the message and became believers (Acts 2:41) and, shortly after, that number rose to 5,000 men (Acts 4:4). In the centre of Acts we have the Jerusalem Council where all the speakers were Christian Jews (Acts 15). When we come to Acts 21 we read of "how many thousands of Jews have believed" (verse 20), and the Greek states *myriads*, i.e. tens of thousands. And Acts ends with Paul debating with the Jewish leaders in Rome, some of whom believed (Acts 28:17,24).

In fact words pertaining to the people of Israel – words like Israel, Jew, Hebrew, Abraham, Isaac, Jacob, Moses, circumcise – occur over 130 times in the Acts of the Apostles alone. It has been argued that although the Acts of the Apostles starts off with the Jews being dominant, over the course of the book, they lose that prominent position. However, the distribution of those words in the *NIV* is approximately as follows:

Acts chapters	Israel (ite)	Jew(s)(ess)(ish)	Greek(s)	Gentile(s)
1-7	13	6	0	1
8-14	6	20	1	14
15-21	1	35	12	13
22-28	1	26	0	5

This table would imply that although the Gentile role did increase during the time covered by the Acts of the Apostles, the Jews were still predominant. And, as we noted above, nine letters were specifically addressed to Christian Jews, and the other six included sections for them.

Similarly, if we consider the number of references to the Mosaic Law (Greek *nomos*) there are approximately 30 references in the Gospels but over 150 in the Acts of the Apostles and the letters written during that time. (Figures are taken from the *Englishman's Greek Concordance of the New Testament*.)

Books or Letters	Number of references to *nomos*
The four Gospels	31
The Acts of the Apostles	19
The nine Jewish letters	22
Paul's six earlier letters (Galatians; 1 & 2 Thessalonians; 1 & 2 Corinthians; Romans)	112

It is therefore clear that the Law was an important issue during the time covered by the Acts of the Apostles. We will discover that it was the will of God for the Jewish Christians of that time to continue following the Mosaic Law and obeying its commandments. This was exemplified in the life of the Apostle Paul, who was a Jew and who, during the Acts of the Apostles, clearly kept the Law. For example:

- On a number of occasions we read of him keeping the Sabbath. (Acts 13:14; 16:13; 17:2; 18:4)
- He practised circumcision on Jews. (Acts 16:3)
- He undertook Nazirite vows. (Acts 18:18; 21:22-26; see Numbers 6:18)
- He observed Jewish Feasts. (Unleavened Bread, Acts 20:6; Pentecost, Acts 20:16)
- He respected the office of the High Priest. (Acts 23:5; Exodus 22:28)
- He was concerned about being ceremonially clean in the temple. (Acts 24:18)

So neither the people of Israel nor the Law of Moses was 'done away with' at the cross. Both are very much in evidence during the thirty or so years following Christ's resurrection and ascension. That being the case, we will consider first the Jewish Christians at the time the book of Acts was written. What was the will of God for them at that time?

The will of God for Jewish Christians during the Acts Period

Acts 11:27-30 records Paul and Barnabas being sent to Jerusalem and Galatians 2 indicates what they did there. There was a meeting between Paul and Barnabas, on the one hand, and Peter, James and John on the other. The result of that meeting was an agreement.

> James, Peter and John, those reputed to be pillars, gave me and Barnabas the right hand of fellowship when they recognised the grace given to me. They agreed that we should go to the Gentiles, and they to the Jews. (Galatians 2:9)

So, turning first to the writings of Peter, James and John, what did they have to say about God's will for the people they wrote to, the Jewish Christians of the Acts period?

> I write to you, fathers, because you have known him who is from the beginning. I write to you, young men, because you are strong, and the word of God lives in you, and you have overcome the evil one. Do not love the world or anything in the world. If anyone loves the world, the love of the Father is not in him. For everything in the world - the cravings of sinful man, the lust of his eyes and the boasting of what he has and does - comes not from the Father but from the world. The world and its desires pass away, but the man who does the will of God lives forever. (1 John 2:14-17)

For John's readers, doing the will of God involved turning their backs on the world and the things of the world. John is very clear that love of the world is inconsistent with love of the Father. The aspects of "the world" that John points out here reflect teaching in the Old Testament – cravings and lust were condemned by the tenth commandment, not to covet, while boastfulness and pride were shown by the

> For John's readers, doing the will of God involved turning their backs on the world and the things of the world.

writers of Proverbs to be contrary to God's will – e.g. "The Lord detests all the proud of heart" (Proverbs 16:5).

The young men who overcame the evil one were strengthened by the word of God, which lived in them. What does John mean by the "Word of God" in this context? Obviously, this would include the Old Testament scriptures, but beyond that, John also had in mind the teachings of the Lord Jesus in His earthly ministry. As John says in the opening chapter of his first epistle:

> That which was from the beginning, which we have heard, which we have seen with our eyes, which we have looked at and our hands have touched – this we proclaim concerning the Word of life ... We proclaim to you what we have seen and heard, so that you also may have fellowship with us. And our fellowship is with the Father and with his Son, Jesus Christ. (1 John 1:1, 3)

John was proclaiming the Word – in the person and teaching of the Lord Jesus. As he warns his readers in his second epistle:

> Anyone who runs ahead and does not continue in the teaching of Christ does not have God; whoever continues in the teaching has both the Father and the Son. (2 John 9)

This message echoes what Christ said in Matthew 7:21: "Not everyone who says to me, 'Lord, Lord,' will enter the kingdom of heaven, but only he who does the will of my Father who is in heaven." Having said this, the Lord immediately goes on to speak of the wise man who "hears these words of mine and puts them into practice" (Matthew 7:24).

The will of the Father, then, is that believers should obey the commands of the Lord Jesus Christ. As John says in his first epistle:

> ... this is his (God's) command: to believe in the name of his Son, Jesus Christ, and to love one another as he commanded us.

Those who obey his commands live in him, and he in them. (1 John 3:23-24)

We can therefore see the threads of the Lord's teaching in the Gospels being picked up in the epistles of the Acts period. John has warned his readers not to love the world. Peter has something similar to say:

> Dear friends, I urge you, as aliens and strangers in the world, to abstain from sinful desires, which war against your soul. Live such good lives among the pagans that, though they accuse you of doing wrong, they may see your good deeds and glorify God on the day he visits us. Submit yourselves for the Lord's sake to every authority instituted among men: whether to the king, as the supreme authority, or to governors, who are sent by him to punish those who do wrong and to commend those who do right. For it is God's will that by doing good you should silence the ignorant talk of foolish men. Live as free men, but do not use your freedom as a cover-up for evil; live as servants of God. Show proper respect to everyone: Love the brotherhood of believers, fear God, honour the king. Slaves, submit yourselves to your masters with all respect, not only to those who are good and considerate, but also to those who are harsh. For it is commendable if a man bears up under the pain of unjust suffering because he is conscious of God. But how is it to your credit if you receive a beating for doing wrong and endure it? But if you suffer for doing good and you endure it, this is commendable before God. (1 Peter 2:11-20)

Here is a clear testimony that the will of God for the Jewish Christians of the Acts Period was to do good. By living good lives they would silence their critics. The details of the passage tell us what good needs to be done. We see, again, it is all very moral and practical, and in harmony with the Law of Moses and Christ's commands to love not only

Here is a clear testimony that the will of God for the Jewish Christians of the Acts Period was to do good.

God and their neighbours, but also their fellow-Christians ("the brotherhood of believers"). Peter returns to the theme of how to live in the next chapter.

> But in your hearts set apart Christ as Lord. Always be prepared to give an answer to everyone who asks you to give the reason for the hope that you have. But do this with gentleness and respect, keeping a clear conscience, so that those who speak maliciously against your good behaviour in Christ may be ashamed of their slander. It is better, if it is God's will, to suffer for doing good than for doing evil. For Christ died for sins once for all, the righteous for the unrighteous, to bring you to God. He was put to death in the body but made alive by the Spirit. (1 Peter 3:15-18)

Here there is an emphasis on being gentle, treating others with respect, having a clear conscience and doing good. However, the theme of 'suffering' comes in as well and seemingly it might be God's will for a person to suffer for doing good. This is what happened to Christ, and it could, and did, happen to some of those Jewish Christians during the Acts period.

> So then, those who suffer according to God's will should commit themselves to their faithful Creator and continue to do good. (1 Peter 4:19)

Whatever happened to them, good or bad, ease or suffering, it was God's will for them to continue to do good. Hebrews has more to say on the theme of suffering.

> Remember those earlier days after you had received the light, when you stood your ground in a great contest in the face of suffering. Sometimes you were publicly exposed to insult and persecution; at other times you stood side by side with those who were so treated. You sympathized with those in prison and

joyfully accepted the confiscation of your property, because you knew that you yourselves had better and lasting possessions. So do not throw away your confidence; it will be richly rewarded. You need to persevere so that when you have done the will of God, you will receive what he has promised. (Hebrews 10:32-36)

It would seem that the will of God for these Jewish Christians at that time included:

- facing the suffering, public insults and persecution they would receive from being Christians;
- standing side by side with others who were treated similarly and sympathise with Jewish Christians in prison; (see Christ's words in Matthew 25:34-36)
- 'joyfully' accepting the confiscation of their property;
- keeping up their confidence and perseverance.

They should do so because they are to be rewarded in eternal life, which has far better and longer-lasting possessions, and this echoes the words of Christ.

"Do not store up for yourselves treasures on earth, where moth and rust destroy, and where thieves break in and steal. But store up for yourselves treasures in heaven, where moth and rust do not destroy, and where thieves do not break in and steal. For where your treasure is, there your heart will be also." (Matthew 6:19-21; see also Luke 12:33, 34)

Also, this suffering is, again, linked by Peter to that of Christ:

Therefore, since Christ suffered in his body, arm yourselves also with the same attitude, because he who has suffered in his body is done with sin. As a result, he does not live the rest of his earthly life for evil human desires, but rather for the will of

God. For you have spent enough time in the past doing what pagans choose to do - living in debauchery, lust, drunkenness, orgies, carousing and detestable idolatry. They think it strange that you do not plunge with them into the same flood of dissipation, and they heap abuse on you. But they will have to give account to him who is ready to judge the living and the dead. (1 Peter 4:1-5)

Peter wrote to the Jewish dispersion, those 'scattered' throughout various parts of the Roman Empire (1 Peter 1:1; 2 Peter 3:1). Sadly, some of these Jews had fallen away from the moral standards of the Law of Moses and into a pagan, immoral lifestyle. The will of God for these people was to leave that lifestyle – leave debauchery, lust, drunkenness, orgies, carousing and idolatry – and to put up with the scorn from those who continued in such things, and any suffering which might result. Again, we see the will of God is concerned with the moral lifestyle of the person.

> The will of God for these people was to leave that lifestyle – leave debauchery, lust, drunkenness, orgies, carousing and idolatry – and to put up with the scorn from those who continued in such things, and any suffering which might result.

The last reference in this section to the will of God highlights their need to acknowledge that the Lord is sovereign, and to continue to do good.

Now listen, you who say, "Today or tomorrow we will go to this or that city, spend a year there, carry on business and make money." Why, you do not even know what will happen tomorrow. What is your life? You are a mist that appears for a little while and then vanishes. Instead, you ought to say, "If it is the Lord's will, we will live and do this or that." As it is, you boast and brag. All such boasting is evil. Anyone, then, who knows the good he ought to do and doesn't do it, sins. (James 4:13-17)

This desire to "make money" is, again, reminiscent of Christ's teaching on the parable of the rich fool, who boasted and bragged about his possessions (Luke 12:16-21).

James wrote to Jewish Christians, to those who belonged to "the twelve tribes scattered among the nations" (James 1:1). Not only does he tell them they need to do good, and that anyone "who knows the good he ought to do and doesn't do it, sins", he also makes it clear that "faith by itself, if it is not accompanied by action, is dead" (James 2:17). John the Baptist challenged people to "produce fruit in keeping with repentance" (Matthew 3:8). Christ, himself, stated that "By their fruit you will recognize them ... every good tree bears good fruit" (Matthew 7:16-17). And James stated:

> Religion that God our Father accepts as pure and faultless is this: to look after orphans and widows in their distress and to keep oneself from being polluted by the world. (James 1:27; and note 2:1-4, 15)

In James 4:16 he states that boasting and bragging is evil, and he spends a long section warning of the dangers of not controlling the tongue (James 3:3-12). He contrasts the boasting and cursing which comes from the same tongue that praises God (James 3:5, 9-10). This is highly inconsistent and James states very bluntly "This should not be" (James 3:10).

He also contrasts human wisdom – which harbours bitter envy and selfish ambition and which results in disorder and evil practice – with heavenly wisdom – which is peace-loving, considerate, submissive, full of mercy, impartial and sincere. Such wisdom raises a harvest of righteousness (James 3:13-18). James gives a great deal of practical advice to these Jewish Christians, but what is his attitude towards the Law?

The place of the Law

Much of the teaching of James is tailored towards the environment in which these first century Jewish Christians were living, but there is an assumption in his writings that observing the Law is still important. For example in James 2:8-13 we read:

> If you really keep the royal law found in Scripture, "Love your neighbour as yourself," you are doing right. But if you show favouritism, you sin and are convicted by the law as lawbreakers. For whoever keeps the whole law and yet stumbles at just one point is guilty of breaking all of it. For he who said, "Do not commit adultery," also said, "Do not murder." If you do not commit adultery but do commit murder, you have become a lawbreaker. Speak and act as those who are going to be judged by the law that gives freedom, because judgment without mercy will be shown to anyone who has not been merciful. Mercy triumphs over judgment!

James has been urging his readers not to discriminate against the poor and vulnerable in society. Instead they are to show 'mercy' to them. Here James is echoing the instructions of the prophet Zechariah:

> James urged his readers not to discriminate against the poor and vulnerable in society. Instead show them 'mercy'.

> This is what the Lord Almighty says: "Administer true justice; show mercy and compassion to one another. Do not oppress the widow or the fatherless, the alien or the poor. In your hearts do not think evil of each other." (Zechariah 7:9-10)

His warning that these Jewish Christians will not be shown mercy by God if they fail to show mercy to others resonates with the Lord's teaching, in Matthew 18:21-35, in His parable of the unmerciful servant. James's readers were still expected to keep that Law.

But it was not only in failing to show mercy that they were in danger of breaking the Law. James explained that, if they judge or speak against one another, they were speaking against the Law:

> Brothers, do not slander one another. Anyone who speaks against his brother or judges him speaks against the law and judges it. When you judge the law, you are not keeping it, but sitting in judgment on it. There is only one Lawgiver and Judge, the one who is able to save and destroy. But you – who are you to judge your neighbour? (James 4:11-12)

As with the issue of failing to show mercy, James is repeating the Lord's teaching in Matthew 7:1-5 that those who judge others are in danger of being judged in turn, under the Law (see also Matthew 5:22). John, in his first epistle, also indicates the importance of the Law by suggesting that all sin involves breaking the Law.

> Everyone who sins breaks the law; in fact, sin is lawlessness. (1 John 3:4)

Throughout his letter James is asking a lot from these Jewish Christians. Would they be able to deliver it in their own strength?

Extra help

We don't need to know much about first century Christianity to know how difficult it was for those early Christians. However, the Jewish Christians had it doubly difficult. Not only did they suffer at the hands of the Gentile authorities, but they also suffered dreadfully from their own leaders, those Jews who did not believe in Jesus.

At the start of Acts we read of Peter and John being imprisoned and beaten by the Jewish leadership (Acts 4:3; 5:18, 40). Paul wrote of the persecution and problems he experienced in such places as 2 Corinthians 11:23-26.

At the end of Acts Josephus records the high priest having James and others stoned to death in Jerusalem (*Antiquities of the Jews*; 20,9,1). How did those Jewish Christians cope with their persecution? When He was on earth Christ told them:

> "And I will ask the Father, and he will give you another Counsellor to be with you forever— the Spirit of truth. The world cannot accept him, because it neither sees him nor knows him. But you know him, for he lives with you and will be in you. I will not leave you as orphans; I will come to you ... But the Counsellor, the Holy Spirit, whom the Father will send in my name, will teach you all things and will remind you of everything I have said to you." (John 14:16-18,26)

After His resurrection the Lord gave them His Holy Spirit (John 20:22) and on the Day of Pentecost the Holy Spirit came upon all the Jewish Christians gathered there in Jerusalem (Acts 2). The Spirit empowered them and enabled them, encouraged them and strengthened them, comforted and counselled them.

It was also through the Holy Spirit that the Lord gave them other helps, including prophets (1 Corinthians 12). At that time, the Apostles may have had all the gifts of the Spirit (2 Corinthians 12:12), but there were some people in those churches of the Acts period who also had the gift of prophecy. Just like the Old Testament prophets, their main job was to speak on behalf of God; to exhort and encourage the people to obey God, by reminding them of what He had done in the past and telling them what would happen in the future. God may have communicated to them by voice or by visions, as in the Old Testament. He did this with people like:

- Peter: who had a vision and who was spoken to by the Holy Spirit (Acts 10:17,19);
- Paul: who had many visions and directions (e.g. Acts 16:7,8; 18:9; 23:11)

In this way He directed them and informed them of His will.

We read of such prophets in Acts 11:27 and one of them, named Agabus, did foretell of a great famine which was to come, and this prophecy enabled the Jewish Christians in Judea to prepare for it (Acts 11:28-29). He also prophesied of Paul's betrayal by the Jews in Jerusalem (Acts 21:10-11). And we read of other prophets in such places as Acts 13:1 and 15:32, and we read of women prophets in Acts 21:9 and 1 Corinthians 11:5.

In summary...

We have looked at relevant references in the Acts of the Apostles, and in those letters written during the time covered by the Acts of the Apostles which were written specifically to Jewish Christians. We saw that the will of God for them was primarily concerned with ethical and moral matters, and for the believers not to conform to the ways of this world. The writers of the epistles sought to put into practice much of the Lord's teaching and personal example given during His earthly ministry to Israel. All of this was in harmony with the Mosaic Law, but we shall look further at this Law and its role for these people a little later.

However, the will of God also dealt with suffering that may result from being a Christian, and instructed them through the teaching of the Apostles how to cope with any persecution. We also saw that at times, just like in the Old Testament, visions and revelations were given to certain individuals to guide them and others but again, as in the Old Testament, these were primarily for the leaders.

But what about the other letters written during this time? We next turn to see what advice Paul gave to the Jewish and Gentile Christians during the time covered by the Acts of the Apostles. Was his advice different from that given by James, Peter and John?

The Will of God: Past and Present   103

Chapter 10
The will of God in Paul's Acts Period writing:
To Jewish and Gentile Christians

We mentioned earlier the meeting between Paul and Barnabas, on the one hand, and Peter, James and John, on the other (Galatians 2:9). They agreed that Paul and Barnabas were to go to the 'Gentiles'. However, we would be wrong to think of this ethnically – i.e. excluding the Jewish people. The word for 'Gentiles' is the Greek *ethnoi* and can be translated 'nations.' Paul was commissioned by Christ to carry His name "before the Gentiles and their kings and before the people of Israel" (Acts 9:15). So when Paul went to the 'Nations' he always went first to the Jewish synagogues before he preached to Gentiles in market places or lecture halls. The churches he established were therefore a mixture of Jewish and Gentile Christians.

As we have seen, the Jewish Christians were steeped in the Law of Moses. The Gentile Christians were different; some of the educated ones might have read the Greek philosophers but others were uneducated pagans, straight from the Greek temples and market places. In the letters to the Romans, Galatians, Corinthians and Thessalonians, Paul wrote

> The Gentile Christians were different; some of the educated ones migh have read the Greek philosophers but others were uneducated pagans, straight from the Greek temples and market places.

to churches which contained both Jewish and Gentile Christians.

In some of these letters, issues pertaining to the Law of Moses are quite dominant. For example 1 Corinthians has 9 references to the Law (*nomos*), Galatians has about 32, and Romans has over 70. In Galatians and Romans in particular, Paul is at pains to point out that neither circumcision nor obedience to the Mosaic Law was necessary for salvation. After all, "Abraham believed God, and it was credited to him as righteousness" (Genesis 15:6; Romans 4:3). This was before

Abraham was circumcised (Genesis 17:24; Romans 4:10) and hundreds of years before the Law was given through Moses.

However, if we look through these letters that Paul wrote to the Jewish and Gentile Christians of the Acts Period, we shall see that the main issues of God's will for both groups were to do with morality and the way they lived their lives. Paul deals with a number of practical aspects of Christian living.

Sexual morality

> Finally, brothers, we instructed you how to live in order to please God, as in fact you are living. Now we ask you and urge you in the Lord Jesus to do this more and more. For you know what instructions we gave you by the authority of the Lord Jesus. It is God's will that you should be sanctified: that you should avoid sexual immorality; that each of you should learn to control his own body in a way that is holy and honourable, not in passionate lust like the heathen, who do not know God; and that in this matter no-one should wrong his brother or take advantage of him. The Lord will punish men for all such sins, as we have already told you and warned you. For God did not call us to be impure, but to live a holy life. Therefore, he who rejects this instruction does not reject man but God, who gives you his Holy Spirit. (1 Thessalonians 4:1-8)

This passage makes it very clear that to please God they needed to live their lives in a certain way. They needed to follow the instructions given them by Paul which he gave them while he was with them and which were now contained in his letters. The will of God was for them to be sanctified and live holy lives. Thus they needed to get rid of what was impure and to avoid sexual immorality: that is, what is sexually immoral according to *Scripture*, not according to society.

Mutual support

Now we ask you, brothers, to respect those who work hard among you, who are over you in the Lord and who admonish you. Hold them in the highest regard in love because of their work. Live in peace with each other. And we urge you, brothers, warn those who are idle, encourage the timid, help the weak, be patient with everyone. Make sure that nobody pays back wrong for wrong, but always try to be kind to each other and to everyone else. Be joyful always; pray continually; give thanks in all circumstances, for this is God's will for you in Christ Jesus. (1 Thessalonians 5:12-18)

This passage in 1 Thessalonians paints a wonderful picture of the positive relationships that should exist in the Christian community. Respect and support is offered to leadership; those who are weak are encouraged; those who are lazy are admonished; the overall attitude to one another is one of tolerance and forgiveness and the atmosphere in the fellowship is one of joy and thankfulness to the Lord.

> The overall attitude to one another is one of tolerance and forgiveness and the atmosphere in the fellowship is one of joy and thankfulness to the Lord.

The teaching in this section is very similar to what Peter and others said to the Jewish Christians to whom they wrote. See, for example, 1 Peter 4:1-5:

Therefore, since Christ suffered in his body, arm yourselves also with the same attitude, because he who has suffered in his body is done with sin. As a result, he does not live the rest of his earthly life for evil human desires, but rather for the will of God. For you have spent enough time in the past doing what pagans choose to do—living in debauchery, lust, drunkenness, orgies, carousing and detestable idolatry. They think it strange that you do not plunge with them into the same flood of dissipation, and they heap abuse on you. But they will have to give account to him who is ready to judge the living and the dead.

So on matters of morality, love and attitude, there is little difference between what Paul wrote and what was said in the letters addressed specifically to Jewish Christians. However, understandably, Paul had to emphasise sexual ethics more strongly because of the low morality of some of the Gentile pagans and the permissiveness of the Greco-Roman world.

Generosity

We read also that 'giving' was part of the will of God. The Macedonian churches were particularly strong in this, as Paul told the Corinthians in his attempt to encourage them to give to the collection for the poor Jewish Christians in Jerusalem who were struggling with a famine.

> And now, brothers, we want you to know about the grace that God has given the Macedonian churches. Out of the most severe trial, their overflowing joy and their extreme poverty welled up in rich generosity. For I testify that they gave as much as they were able, and even beyond their ability. Entirely on their own, they urgently pleaded with us for the privilege of sharing in this service to the saints. And they did not do as we expected, but they gave themselves first to the Lord and then to us in keeping with God's will. So we urged Titus, since he had earlier made a beginning, to bring also to completion this act of grace on your part. (2 Corinthians 8:1-6)

God's way and the world's

When writing to the Romans Paul told them that they needed to live holy and pleasing lives, not conforming to the pattern of this world. In this he may have been issuing a challenge. If they lived holy and pleasing lives they would see how much better life actually was. This would enable them to *test* the will of God and *prove* to themselves that it was the best way to live.

> Therefore, I urge you, brothers, in view of God's mercy, to offer your bodies as living sacrifices, holy and pleasing to God - this is your spiritual act of worship. Do not conform any longer to the pattern of this world, but be transformed by the renewing of your mind. Then you will be able to test and approve what God's will is - his good, pleasing and perfect will. For by the grace given me I say to every one of you: Do not think of yourself more highly than you ought, but rather think of yourself with sober judgment, in accordance with the measure of faith God has given you. (Romans 12:1-3)

They were not to think too highly of themselves; meekness and humility, rather than pomp and pride, was the order of the day.

He also told the Romans that it was the will of God for the Holy Spirit to intercede on their behalf, especially when they were having problems with knowing what to pray for.

> In the same way, the Spirit helps us in our weakness. We do not know what we ought to pray for, but the Spirit himself intercedes for us with groans that words cannot express. And he who searches our hearts knows the mind of the Spirit, because the Spirit intercedes for the saints in accordance with God's will. And we know that in all things God works for the good of those who love him, who have been called according to his purpose. (Romans 8:26-28)

And of course, any prayer offered by the Spirit when He intercedes on the believer's behalf would be in accordance with God's will.

Paul and the will of God

We saw earlier, when dealing with the Jews in the Old Testament, that the will of God for the highest and the lowest in the land was to 'fully' obey the Law of Moses. However, for the leaders there were extra responsibilities and at times they needed special guidance on issues not connected with the Law of Moses, maybe political decisions relating to other countries. This was supplied either by the leader going to the priest who had the Urim and Thummim, or by the Lord speaking to someone, maybe the king or a prophet, or giving them a vision.

In the New Testament the Apostles had specific local issues to deal with, over and above following the Law and living a good and moral life. On such issues there was no clear guidance in the Old Testament Scriptures or in the Lord's teaching. Thus at times direct guidance as to the will of God on these matters was given to the Apostles by the Holy Spirit, Himself. He may have spoken directly to them or they may have been given a vision. This was certainly the case not only with Paul, as we shall see, but also with other Apostles.

When the Lord wanted Peter to visit the God-fearing Gentile Cornelius, Peter was given a vision, after which the Holy Spirit spoke directly to him (Acts 10:9-16 and note vs 19-20). Similarly an angel of the Lord was sent to direct Philip into the path of the Ethiopian eunuch (Acts 8:26), and the Holy Spirit Himself spoke to the leaders of the church at Antioch. He instructed them to set apart Paul and Barnabas, and these two then set off on their first missionary journey (Acts 13:1-3). In the Old Testament the Lord, at times, had spoken directly to a leader, the Judge, the King or the prophet. What we have here, in the Acts period, is something quite similar.

Paul had a great desire to visit the Roman Christians and twice mentioned this to them, once at the start of his letter to the Romans, and again near the end.

> In the Old Testament the Lord, at times, had spoken directly to a leader, the Judge, the King or the prophet. What we have here, in the Acts period, is something quite similar.

First, I thank my God through Jesus Christ for all of you, because your faith is being reported all over the world. God, whom I serve with my whole heart in preaching the gospel of his Son, is my witness how constantly I remember you in my prayers at all times; and I pray that now at last by God's will the way may be opened for me to come to you. (Romans 1:8-10)

Pray that I may be rescued from the unbelievers in Judea and that my service in Jerusalem may be acceptable to the saints there, so that by God's will I may come to you with joy and together with you be refreshed. (Romans 15:31-32)

Paul wanted to go to Rome, but it had to be the will of God for him to do so.

On his second missionary journey Paul wanted to visit first Asia and then Bithynia but, in some way, the Holy Spirit prevented him from doing so. We read:

Paul and his companions travelled throughout the region of Phrygia and Galatia, having been kept by the Holy Spirit from preaching the word in the province of Asia. When they came to the border of Mysia, they tried to enter Bithynia, but the Spirit of Jesus would not allow them to. So they passed by Mysia and went down to Troas. (Acts 16:6-8)

It would seem it was not the will of God for Paul to go into either Asia or Bithynia. Somehow he was prevented and eventually was given a vision which led him to Philippi, taking the gospel into Macedonia (Acts 16:9-10).

Paul did eventually reach Rome, but the way in which he got there was not the way he initially expected.

After we had been there a number of days, a prophet named Agabus came down from Judea. Coming over to us, he took

Paul's belt, tied his own hands and feet with it and said, "The Holy Spirit says, 'In this way the Jews of Jerusalem will bind the owner of this belt and will hand him over to the Gentiles.'" When we heard this, we and the people there pleaded with Paul not to go up to Jerusalem. Then Paul answered, "Why are you weeping and breaking my heart? I am ready not only to be bound, but also to die in Jerusalem for the name of the Lord Jesus." When he would not be dissuaded, we gave up and said, "The Lord's will be done." After this, we got ready and went up to Jerusalem. (Acts 21:10-15)

Agabus prophesied that Paul was to be handed over to the Gentiles, and although initially the people tried to dissuade Paul from going to Jerusalem, in the vain hope that somehow the fulfilment of this prophecy could be avoided, in the end they concluded that there was no point in doing so; this was the will of God.

Paul took a similar line when he visited the saints in Ephesus, on his way back to Jerusalem on his second missionary journey.

When they asked him to spend more time with them, he declined. But as he left, he promised, "I will come back if it is God's will." Then he set sail from Ephesus. (Acts 18:20-21)

It seems it was the will of God for Paul to return, for he visited them, and stayed two years or so, on his third missionary journey. Also, on the return journey to Jerusalem, he called in at Miletus and sent for the Ephesian elders. There he said to them:

"Now I know that none of you among whom I have gone about preaching the kingdom will ever see me again. Therefore, I declare to you today that I am innocent of the blood of all men. For I have not hesitated to proclaim to you the whole will of God." (Acts 20:25-27)

Thus what Paul taught them, including instructions on how to grow in their knowledge of God as well as matters of moral, ethical and loving behaviour, was the will of God.

Paul had a very special place in God's plan for mankind. He was chosen to be the 'Apostle to the Gentiles' by the will of God (Romans 11:13; 1 Corinthians 1:1; 2 Corinthians 1:1; Galatians 1:15-16; 2:8-9). Sometimes where he went and what he did was subject to the will of God. In those circumstances he was occasionally directed by the Holy Spirit or by visions. However, we should be wary of extending such specific instructions to the ordinary Christians to whom he wrote.

An apostle, like a king in the Old Testament, had greater responsibilities. The way in which God, at times, made known His specific will for where He wanted the Apostle Paul to go and preach Christ should not be extended to those who were not in positions of leadership. In fact there is no record in the Acts of the Apostles, or any of the epistles and letters, of any ordinary Christian receiving instructions as to whether he should or should not go somewhere or other. Where they lived, and where they went, and who they saw, was their own personal decision. Aquila and Priscilla, tentmakers like Paul (Acts 18:2, 3), for example, appear to have travelled extensively, offering hospitality to Paul and others wherever they went. Aquila was a native of Pontus, but the couple were living in Rome when Claudius expelled all the Jews from the city in AD 49. They then went to Corinth where they met Paul. When he left Corinth, they came with him as far as Ephesus (Acts 18:19). Romans 16:3 indicates that they were subsequently back in Rome.

We should also point out that, even with respect to the Apostles, such specific instructions and guidance by the Holy Spirit or by visions were given *only in relation to the Lord's work*, and not in relation to other aspects of their lives.

In summary...

We have considered the relevant references in Paul's earlier letters, those written to churches which were a mixture of Jewish and Gentile Christians. We saw that Paul wanted them to live lives which pleased God. This could be achieved by living moral, loving lives, abstaining from the permissiveness of the surrounding society, and caring for fellow Christians.

However, we note that there are no verses in the Acts of the Apostles or any of the epistles which suggest that the ordinary Christians should receive, or even seek for, such specific guidance. Although Paul himself, at times had specific guidance from the Holy Spirit, when it comes to the people to whom he wrote, the emphasis was on how they lived their lives, what they should do and what they should not do, and their love and care for others. The issue was what sort of people they should be. That was the will of God for them.

The emphasis in the teaching of the apostles of this time was that Christians, whether Jews or Gentiles, should behave in a way that was pleasing to the Lord. Their lives should be characterised by love, the fruit of the Holy Spirit, and by a moral outlook that stood in stark contrast to the pagan society around them. We have noted references to the Law of Moses, which indicate that it underpinned much of the teaching of the Apostles. But what, exactly, was the position of the Law during the Acts period? This will be considered in the next chapter.

Chapter 11
The Law of Moses during the Acts Period

We have seen the dominant role the Law of Moses played with respect to the will of God. From the time God gave it through Moses, and throughout the rest of the Old Testament, and into the Gospel Period, to fully obey the Law of Moses was the will of God. We hinted earlier that this was also the will of God for the Jewish Christians during the Acts Period. However, some Christians challenge this and state that at the Cross the Law was abolished for the Jews and that Christian Jews no longer needed to observe it. We need to investigate this and see whether or not they did so.

> Some Christians state that at the Cross the Law was abolished for the Jews and that Christian Jews no longer needed to observe it.

Paul and the Law of Moses

Apart from our Lord Jesus Christ, we have more information about Paul than we have about any other character in the New Testament. If we consider the Apostle Paul during the Acts Period we see him worshipping in the synagogue on the Sabbath. We read the following:

> From Perga they went on to Pisidian Antioch. On *the Sabbath* they entered the synagogue and sat down. After the reading from the Law and the Prophets, the synagogue rulers sent word to them, saying, "Brothers, if you have a message of encouragement for the people, please speak." (Acts 13:14-15)

Paul was there the next Sabbath day also (see verses 42-44) and this was his practice wherever he went - to attend the synagogue. For example at Thessalonica we read:

> *As his custom was*, Paul went into the synagogue, and *on three Sabbath days* he reasoned with them from the Scriptures,

explaining and proving that the Christ had to suffer and rise from the dead. (Acts 17:2-3)

And similarly in Corinth, *"Every Sabbath* he reasoned in the synagogue, trying to persuade Jews and Greeks" (Acts 18:1-4). Even in Philippi, where there was no synagogue, Paul still kept the Sabbath.

> On *the Sabbath* we went outside the city gate to the river, where we expected to find a place of prayer. (Acts 16:13)

The Law of Moses, in Numbers chapter 6, sets out in considerable detail what a Jew must do if he wishes to make a special Nazirite vow before the Lord. During the Acts period we see Paul making this vow on two occasions.

> Paul stayed on in Corinth for some time. Then he left the brothers and sailed for Syria, accompanied by Priscilla and Aquila. Before he sailed, he had his hair cut off at Cenchrea because of *a vow* he had taken. (Acts 18:18)

On the second occasion, he undertook the vow at the request of James, the brother of Jesus who, by this time, was the leader of the church in Jerusalem. Lies had been told about Paul, and James and the elders of the Jerusalem Church wanted the record put straight. This is what he said to Paul:

> They [the Jews in Jerusalem] have been informed that you teach all the Jews who live among the Gentiles to turn away from Moses, telling them not to circumcise their children or live according to our customs. What shall we do? They will certainly hear that you have come, so do what we tell you. There are four men with us who have made *a vow.* Take these men, *join in their purification rites* and pay their expenses, so that they can have their heads shaved. Then everybody will

know there is no truth in these reports about you, but that *you yourself are living in obedience to the law*. (Acts 21:21-24)

And this is exactly what Paul did to show that he, himself, was "living in obedience to the law".

> The next day Paul took the men and purified himself along with them. Then he went to the temple to give notice of the date when the days of purification would end and the offering would be made for each of them. (Acts 21:26)

So here we see both James and the elders of the Jerusalem Church extolling the Law of Moses. Earlier they had told Paul:

> "You see, brother, how many thousands of Jews have believed, and *all of them are zealous for the law*." (Acts 21:20)

So we see not only Paul and James upholding the Law of Moses, but thousands of ordinary Jewish Christians also, as well as the Christian leaders in Jerusalem, which would have included some, if not all, of the Twelve Apostles. Not only did Paul keep the Sabbath day and fulfil the Nazirite vow, with all the purification rites and the offerings of Numbers 6, he also observed the rules of the feast of Unleavened Bread, by not travelling during the period of the Feast.

> These men went on ahead and waited for us at Troas. But we sailed from Philippi after the *Feast of Unleavened Bread*, and five days later joined the others at Troas, where we stayed seven days. (Acts 20:5-6)

In the same chapter, we read of his desire to reach Jerusalem in time to celebrate Pentecost.

> The next day we set sail from there and arrived off Kios. The day after that we crossed over to Samos, and on the following

day arrived at Miletus. Paul had decided to sail past Ephesus to avoid spending time in the province of Asia, for he was in a hurry to reach Jerusalem, if possible, by *the day of Pentecost*. (Acts 20:15-16)

Paul also circumcised Timothy, in accordance with the Law of Moses.

> He came to Derbe and then to Lystra, where a disciple named Timothy lived, whose mother was a Jewess and a believer, but whose father was a Greek. The brothers at Lystra and Iconium spoke well of him. Paul wanted to take him along on the journey, so he *circumcised* him because of the Jews who lived in that area, for they all knew that his father was a Greek. (Acts 16:1-3)

And on one occasion Paul regretted the way he had spoken to the high priest. What he had said had broken the Law of Moses and Paul immediately apologised.

> Paul looked straight at the Sanhedrin and said, "My brothers, I have fulfilled my duty to God in all good conscience to this day." At this the high priest Ananias ordered those standing near Paul to strike him on the mouth. Then Paul said to him, "God will strike you, you whitewashed wall! You sit there to judge me according to the law, yet you yourself violate the law by commanding that I be struck!" Those who were standing near Paul said, "You dare to insult God's high priest?" Paul replied, "Brothers, I did not realize that he was the high priest; for it is written: 'Do not speak evil about the ruler of your people.'" (Acts 23:1-5; see Exodus 22:28)

And on his last visit to Jerusalem Paul was concerned to make sure that he was ceremonially clean, according to the Law of Moses, when he went into the temple.

"After an absence of several years, I came to Jerusalem to bring my people gifts for the poor and to present offerings. I was ceremonially clean when they found me in the temple courts doing this. There was no crowd with me, nor was I involved in any disturbance. (Acts 24:17-18)

There can be little doubt that Paul observed the Law of Moses rigorously, but what about other Jewish Christians? As we have mentioned above, it seems that James, the elders in Jerusalem, and the thousands of Jews who believed, all were zealous for the Law (Acts 21:20).

Gentile Christians and the Law of Moses

At the beginning of Acts there are no Gentile Christians. The first to come on the scene was Cornelius, whom Peter visited. Then some Jewish Christians from Cyprus and Cyrene went to Antioch in Syria and told the Greeks there about the Lord Jesus. In the course of time Paul and Barnabus set off on their first Missionary Journey and visited Cyprus before going up into Galatia. On returning to Antioch in Syria it wasn't long before a serious problem arose. A group of Jewish Christians were teaching that, as well as believing in Christ as their Saviour, the Gentiles had to be circumcised to be saved. This caused Paul to write his letter to the Galatians, and he and Barnabas to have "a sharp dispute and debate" with them (Acts 15:1-2).

> Christian Jews would not be insisting that the Gentiles be circumcised if they were not practising circumcision themselves.

Clearly these Christian Jews would not have been insisting that the Gentiles be circumcised if they had not been practising circumcision themselves. Not only that, their arguments were so strong that the elders of the church at Antioch were not won over by the arguments of Paul and Barnabas, and so referred the issue to the apostles and elders in Jerusalem.

When Paul and Barnabas arrived in Jerusalem they were confronted by another group of Christian Jews. These were Pharisees who had come to believe in Jesus. However, their position was that the Gentiles not only had to believe in Christ, they also had to be circumcised and required to keep the Law of Moses (Acts 15:5).

This whole matter was debated in what has become known as *The Jerusalem Council* and with support from Peter, Paul and Barnabas won the day. The decision of the council, as pronounced by James, shows clearly that although the Gentiles did not have to be circumcised and keep the 'whole' Law of Moses, the Jewish Christians were still following that Law, otherwise there would have been no debate. However, there were four aspects of the Law that the Council did want the Gentiles to observe. James said:

> "It is my judgment, therefore, that we should not make it difficult for the Gentiles who are turning to God. Instead we should write to them, telling them to abstain from food polluted by idols, from sexual immorality, from the meat of strangled animals and from blood." (Acts 15:19-20)

This decision was written in a letter and sent with Silas and Judas Barsabbas to the church at Antioch and, no doubt, other areas received copies (Acts 15:22-29). Years later James referred to this decision. At the end of Paul's third missionary journey we read:

> The next day Paul and the rest of us went to see James, and all the elders were present. Paul greeted them and reported in detail what God had done among the Gentiles through his ministry. When they heard this, they praised God. Then they said to Paul: "You see, brother, how many thousands of Jews have believed, and all of them are zealous for the law. They have been informed that you teach all the Jews who live among the Gentiles to turn away from Moses, telling them not to circumcise their children or live according to our customs. What shall we do? They will certainly hear that you have come,

so do what we tell you. There are four men with us who have made a vow. Take these men, join in their purification rites and pay their expenses, so that they can have their heads shaved. Then everybody will know there is no truth in these reports about you, but that you yourself are living in obedience to the law. As for the Gentile believers, we have written to them our decision that they should abstain from food sacrificed to idols, from blood, from the meat of strangled animals and from sexual immorality." (Acts 21:18-25)

Somehow or other, Paul's activities on his missionary journeys had been misreported or misrepresented in Jerusalem. His teaching of the fact that Gentile Christians need not be circumcised had been distorted and he had been accused of saying *Jewish* Christians need not be

> Paul's teaching that Gentile Christians need not be circumcised had been distorted and he had been accused of saying *Jewish* Christians need not be circumcised.

circumcised. The fact that this inaccuracy caused so much concern shows again that the Jewish Christians not only continued in the Law of Moses, but were, in fact, keen and zealous to do so. As for the Gentiles, James reminded Paul of the decision of the Jerusalem Council that the Gentiles would do well to observe these four rules.

Why these four rules?

In *The New Bible Commentary Revised* (page 992), F F Bruce described these four rules as "The condition laid down for social intercourse." To appreciate this we need to understand a little more deeply what was going on at that time.

According to the Law of Moses, anyone who broke any of these four rules rendered himself ceremonially unclean. However, if a Jew was unclean this prevented him from doing certain things, such as attending Temple worship. Not only that, if a Jew had contact with a person who was unclean, then he, himself, would be rendered unclean by having such contact.

The Law of Moses did not state that all Gentiles were unclean; it depended upon what they did. However, the Pharisees had extended that Law to declare that all Gentiles *per se* were unclean. This was one of the Pharisaic additions to the Law that Peter had to unlearn and God gave him the vision of the sheet coming down from heaven to bring him back to the Mosaic Law (Acts 10:9-20). When Peter reached Cornelius, he said to him:

> "You are well aware that it is against our law [Greek, *athemitos*, custom] for a Jew to associate with a Gentile or visit him. But God has shown me that I should not call any man impure or unclean." (Acts 10:28).

Note first that Peter does not use *nomos*, the Greek word for the Mosaic Law. It had become the 'custom', due to Pharisaic teaching, that the Jews considered all non-Jews as unclean. Peter learnt that according to the Law of Moses, and in the eyes of God, this was not the case. It was not a person's race which made him unclean, it was what that person did.

The decision of the Jerusalem Council seems to have been based partly on the issue of ceremonial cleanness and partly on respect for the sensitive conscience of some Jews who considered certain practices offensive. The decision did not command the Gentiles to be circumcised. Neither did it place them under the Law of Moses. Rather it asked the Gentile Christians to observe the following four rules.

- Not to eat food which had been offered to idols.
- Not to engage in sexual activity outside marriage.
- Not to eat the meat of an animal which had been strangled, as the meat would contain the animal's blood.
- Not to drink blood, or possibly not to come into contact with blood.

Any such activities by Gentile Christians would make it very difficult for the Jewish Christians to have fellowship with them. Some behaviour would be highly offensive whilst other practices would render them unclean according to the Law of Moses. If the Jewish Christians had contact with them, they themselves would become unclean! And if, in turn, they had contact with other Jews, some of whom might not yet be Christians, then they, also, would be unclean. Thus, if Christian Jews had regular contact with Christian Gentiles, the non-Christian Jews would have little or nothing to do with the Christian Jews for fear of becoming unclean themselves. Something had to be done to prevent this situation occurring. Asking the Gentiles to observe these four regulations was the solution. However, it again shows how important the Mosaic Law was to the Christian Jews.

The Mosaic Law and Witnessing

It should not surprise us that the Christian Jews continued in their observance of the Law of Moses. They wanted to witness to non-Christian Jews that Jesus was the Christ (Messiah), the Son of God and their Saviour. However, if the Christian Jew stopped observing the Sabbath, he would have been called a 'Gentile dog' by the non-Christian Jew who kept the Sabbath Law. If a Christian Jewish family had a new baby boy and did not have him circumcised on the eighth day according to the Law of Moses, the non-Christian Jews would have nothing to do with them.

> If a Christian Jewish family had a new baby boy and did not have him circumcised on the eighth day according to the Law of Moses, the non-Christian Jews would have nothing to do with them.

Timothy should have been circumcised on the eighth day, but he was not. Thus Paul took him and circumcised him "because of the Jews in that area". They knew his father was a Greek, and that he had not been circumcised (Acts 16:1-3). Thus they would not have listened to Timothy, and if he had entered the synagogues with Paul, Timothy would have been made to sit at the back with the Gentiles. Therefore, as long as it was God's will for the Jewish Christians to witness to those Jews who were not Christians, it was God's will for the Jewish Christians to observe the Law of Moses. We can see, then, that obeying the Law of Moses for Paul and the other Christian Jews was a practical necessity rather than a legal obligation.

The Law in the Earlier Epistles

Some Christian writers have argued that the scenario above is not correct, that the Law was removed but that the Christian Jews were in error in wanting to retain it. As a result some have accused Paul of being duplicitous, by saying and doing one thing when in the company of leading Jewish Christians, but saying and doing something different when they were not around.

It is an interesting fact that the Bible does not hesitate to record some of the failures of its leading characters. We can think of David's affair with Bathsheba and his dealings with her husband Uriah. We have a number of examples of Peter saying and doing wrong things, and we have Paul and Barnabas disagreeing so strongly over John Mark that they went their separate ways. However, if we consider Peter for example, although on the spur of the moment he might speak or act unwisely, when he had time to reflect he always did the right thing. For example, under pressure in Antioch he refused to eat with Gentiles but on reflection, a little later at the Jerusalem Council, he totally supported Paul (compare Galatians 2:11-16 and Acts 15:7-11).

We must not have the idea that the edict of the Jerusalem Council and the letter to the churches was the end of the matter. Some of those Christian Jews who wanted the Gentiles to be circumcised accepted the decision of the Council, but others did not and we can see Paul still battling with them in the letters he wrote much later, after the end of the Acts Period (see Philippians 3:2; Colossians 2:11; Titus 1:10-11). However, all Christian Jews continued to observe the Law of Moses during the Acts Period.

So in dealing with the various churches to which Paul wrote, he had to try and mediate between these different factions within early Christendom. He needed to get them to consider others and to be tolerant of different practices. For example, in Romans 14:1-15 he wrote:

Accept him whose faith is weak, without passing judgment on disputable matters. One man's faith allows him to eat everything, but another man, whose faith is weak, eats only vegetables. The man who eats everything must not look down on him who does not, and the man who does not eat everything must not condemn the man who does, for God has accepted him. Who are you to judge someone else's servant? To his own master he stands or falls. And he will stand, for the Lord is able to make him stand.

One man considers one day more sacred than another; another man considers every day alike. Each one should be fully convinced in his own mind. He who regards one day as special, does so to the Lord.

He who eats meat, eats to the Lord, for he gives thanks to God; and he who abstains, does so to the Lord and gives thanks to God. For none of us lives to himself alone and none of us dies to himself alone. If we live, we live to the Lord; and if we die, we die to the Lord. So, whether we live or die, we belong to the Lord. For this very reason, Christ died and returned to life so that he might be the Lord of both the dead and the living. You, then, why do you judge your brother? Or why do you look down on your brother? For we will all stand before God's judgment seat. It is written: "'As surely as I live,' says the Lord, 'every knee will bow before me; every tongue will confess to God.'" So then, each of us will give an account of himself to God. Therefore let us stop passing judgment on one another. Instead, make up your mind not to put any stumbling-block or obstacle in your brother's way.

As one who is in the Lord Jesus, I am fully convinced that no food is unclean in itself. But if anyone regards something as unclean, then for him it is unclean. If your brother is distressed because of what you eat, you are no longer acting in love. Do not by your eating destroy your brother for whom Christ died.

There are two issues here: one to do with observing days and the other to do with eating food.

Under the Law of Moses the Jews were told to observe the Sabbath Day and various other holy days. As we have seen, the Jewish Christians continued to do this during the Acts Period. However, the Jerusalem Council said nothing about Gentiles having to keep the Sabbath Day in particular or to observe the Sabbath laws in general. So to the mixed group of Christians in Rome Paul *may* have been saying something like this:

> The Jerusalem Council said nothing about Gentiles having to keep the Sabbath Day or to observe the Sabbath laws in general.

> One man [a Jewish Christian] considers one day more sacred than another; another man [a Gentile Christian] considers every day alike. Each one should be fully convinced in his own mind. He who regards one day as special, does so to the Lord.

Similarly, with respect to meat. Although the Jerusalem Council stated that the Gentiles should not eat the meat of strangled animals, it laid no restriction on their eating pork or various other meats forbidden to the Jews in the Mosaic Law. In this passage which is quite difficult for us, 2,000 years later, to fully understand the precise situation, it is possible that Paul *may* have meant something like the following:

> One man's faith [a Gentile Christian] allows him to eat everything, but another man [a Jewish Christian], whose faith is weak, eats only vegetables. The man who eats everything [a Gentile Christian] must not look down on him who does not [a Jewish Christian], and the man who does not eat everything [a Jewish Christian] must not condemn the man who does [a Gentile Christian].

This sort of situation could arise when Jewish and Gentile Christians ate together. If beef or lamb were served by a Gentile Christian, the cautious Jewish Christian might not have been convinced that the meat of his Gentile host had been killed correctly and so would abstain from taking the meat at the meal and eat just the vegetables. Interestingly, this was the position taken by Daniel and his friends in captivity in Babylon (see Daniel 1:8, 12).

Now Paul goes on to say that "As one who is in the Lord Jesus, I am fully convinced that no food is unclean *in itself*" (Romans 14:14). Here, Paul is not trying to undermine the decision of the Jerusalem Council or go against it, or nullify the Law of Moses. He is simply saying that 'in itself' no food is unclean; that is, there is nothing unhealthy in eating pork or indeed the meat of strangled animals. In this he was echoing the words of our Lord Jesus Christ in Mark 7:18-23[5].

However, the Law of Moses forbade eating pork and the meat of strangled animals. Thus the Jewish Christian should not eat them, but the Jewish Christian should not be overly worried about any Gentile Christian who did. He certainly should not judge and look down upon the Gentile Christian who did, and vice versa. Paul concludes by saying:

> But if anyone regards some-thing as unclean, then for him it is unclean. If your brother is distressed because of what you eat, you are no longer acting in love. Do not by your eating destroy your brother for whom Christ died. (Romans 14:14-15)

However, if a Jewish Christian is distressed by a Gentile Christian eating such meat as pork, would it not be best if the Gentile Christian did not eat that meat? This would be a voluntary abstention out of love for a Christian brother. Thus in this passage Paul is going against neither the Law of Moses for the Jewish Christian nor the four rules of the Jerusalem Council for the Gentile Christian. He is simply suggesting that the Gentile Christian go an extra mile (voluntarily) and he is exhorting both groups not to judge one another.

---

[5] For a full treatment of these verses see pages 118-124 of *40 Problem Passages* by Michael Penny, published by The Open Bible Trust.

Under the Law in the Earlier Letters

A few times in his earlier letters Paul uses the expression 'under the law'. For example:

> Now we know that whatever the law says, it says to those who are under the law, so that every mouth may be silenced and the whole world held accountable to God. Therefore no one will be declared righteous in his sight by observing the law; rather, through the law we become conscious of sin. (Romans 3:19-20)

These verses seem to be addressed to the Jewish Christians in the church at Rome who came from a background of being under the Law. Here he emphasises that observance of the Mosaic Law will not bring righteousness because, as he wrote earlier in verse 10, "There is no-one righteous, not even one." However, Paul stated he was not 'under the law'. What did he mean by this statement?

> Though I am free and belong to no man, I make myself a slave to everyone, to win as many as possible. To the Jews I became like a Jew, to win the Jews. To those under the law I became like one under the law (though I myself am not under the law), so as to win those under the law. To those not having the law I became like one not having the law (though I am not free from God's law but am under Christ's law), so as to win those not having the law. To the weak I became weak, to win the weak. I have become all things to all men so that by all possible means I might save some. (1 Corinthians 9:19-22)

Here Paul stated that he was "not under the law", but then went on to say that he was "not free from God's law" and then added that he was "under Christ's law". There is no doubt that Paul's first century readers knew what he meant, but reference to all these different 'laws' is confusing for 21st century Christians. Some today claim that when Paul stated he was "not under the law" that he no longer needed to keep the

Mosaic Law. Now if that interpretation is true we have a clash between what Paul stated here and what he did, as recorded in the Acts of the Apostles.

1 Corinthians was written on Paul's third missionary journey, during his two year stay at Ephesus (Acts 19). However, after that we see Paul wanting to observe the Feasts of Unleavened Bread and Pentecost (Acts 20:6; 20:16); we see him keeping the Nazirite vow and being concerned about ceremonial cleanness when in the temple (Acts 21:20-26; 24:18). And that Nazirite vow was to show that Paul, himself, was "living in obedience to the law" (Acts 21:24). Thus when Paul stated he was "not under the law" he could not have meant that he was not living in accordance with the Law of Moses. In fact he said he was *"not free* from God's Law", and the Jewish Christians who read that letter would have understood that to refer only to the Law of Moses[6]. Certainly he was "not under the law" for righteousness, of that we can be sure, and that may have been what he meant. He did not *rely* on the Law for righteousness (Galatians 3:10). Paul had learnt this himself, as stated in Philippians 3:6-9:

> ... as for legalistic righteousness, faultless. But whatever was to my profit I now consider loss for the sake of Christ. What is more, I consider everything a loss compared to the surpassing greatness of knowing Christ Jesus my Lord, for whose sake I have lost all things. I consider them rubbish, that I may gain Christ and be found in him, not having a righteousness of my own that comes from the law, but that which is through faith in Christ – the righteousness that comes from God and is by faith.

---

[6] Some point out that Paul said he was under Christ's Law (1 Corinthians 9:21) which they say means he was under the teaching of Christ, not Moses. However, in that very verse, Paul states that "I am not free from God's Law" referring to the Mosaic Law. Also, as we have seen earlier, Christ upheld the Law of Moses and stated that people should obey its commandments. Up until now there had been no revelation from God or instructions from Christ for the Jewish Christians to stop following the Law. That would come, but not yet.

In the eyes of the Pharisaic Jewish community, and in his own eyes before his conversion, Paul was considered righteous. He lived in obedience to the Mosaic Law, and the Pharisaic additions to that Law, to such an extent that he was considered 'faultless' – but not by God! And on the Damascus Road he was to learn of God's righteousness which cannot be earned by good works or an obedience to any law, Mosaic or otherwise. It can only be received as a gift from God.

> ... know that a man is not justified by observing the law, but by faith in Jesus Christ. So we, too, have put our faith in Christ Jesus that we may be justified by faith in Christ and not by observing the law, because by observing the law no-one will be justified. (Galatians 2:16)

> All who *rely* on observing the law are under a curse, for it is written: "Cursed is everyone who does not continue to do everything written in the Book of the Law." Clearly no-one is justified before God by the law, because, "The righteous will live by faith." (Galatians 3:10-11)

Thus salvation was by grace through faith, not by works, not by observing the Law, not by performing rituals. However, Paul did consider Himself under Christ's Law and many have pondered upon what Paul meant by this. One possible explanation is based on:

> One of them, an expert in the law, tested him with this question: "Teacher, which is the greatest commandment in the Law?" Jesus replied: "'Love the Lord your God with all your heart and with all your soul and with all your mind.' This is the first and greatest commandment. And the second is like it: 'Love your neighbour as yourself.' All the Law and the Prophets hang on these two commandments." (Matthew 22:35-40)

The essence of the Law of Moses was love for God and neighbour. Christ extended this to loving fellow-Christians and loving enemies.

Paul states something similar in Galatians 5:22-23: "But the fruit of the Spirit is love, joy, peace, patience, kindness, goodness, faithfulness, gentleness and self-control. Against such things there is no law."

If people have love for others, if they exhibit the fruit of the Spirit to those whom they meet, such people do not need the Law of Moses or any other law. They will automatically do the right thing and live in accordance with practical requirements of the Mosaic Law and Christ's Law.

Paul's credibility

Paul wrote a number of things in 1 Corinthians 9:19-22 which have been greatly misunderstood.

> To the Jews I became like a Jew, to win the Jews.
> To those under the law I became like one under the law.
> To those not having the law I became like one not having the law.

Some have suggested that these statements show that Paul kept the Mosaic Law when he was in the company of Jews, but that he did not bother with it when in the company of Gentiles! This would imply lack of integrity on the part of Paul, and it would also be very foolish. The Gentiles whom Paul met were in churches which, during the time covered by the Acts of the Apostles, contained many Jewish Christians, some of whom were in leadership positions. If Paul was so inconsistent, it would soon become obvious and he would lose his credibility, and his authority.

In the Acts of the Apostles, we have clear examples of how Paul dealt differently with Jews and Gentiles. It was not in his behaviour and how he conducted himself with respect to the Law of Moses; it was in what he said and the way in which he said it. For example compare and contrast Paul's speech in the synagogue at Antioch, as recorded in Acts 13:26-41, with the one he made in Athens, Acts 17:22-31. The former was made to Jews and God-fearing Gentiles who attended the synagogue and who knew the Scriptures and who treated them as the Word of God. The latter was made to pagan Gentile philosophers who knew nothing of the Jewish Scriptures and, even if any had read them, they did not consider them to carry any weight or authority. In the synagogue in Antioch we have Paul being a Jew to a Jew; he was like one under the Law because they were under the Law. However, the Athenians were not under the Mosaic Law and so Paul did not support his arguments with quotations from the Law or any other part of the Scriptures. In both approaches his aim was the same: "I have become all things to all men so that by all possible means I might save some" (1 Corinthians 9:22).

In summary...

For the Christian Jews of the Acts period observance of the Law of Moses was an important part of the will of God. We have seen that their character, too, was important to God; He wanted them to live moral lives, and to be loving and caring towards others. This was also true of the Gentile Christians of that time. They did not observe the Sabbath and did not practise circumcision and the ceremonial part of the Mosaic Law and much else. However, being of good character, living moral lives, and observing the four rules laid out by the Jerusalem Council: that was the will of God for them.

Paul also introduced a new dimension to the will of God. A Gentile Christian might be free to eat what he chose, but he needed to consider the feelings of others. If eating meat would cause his Christian brother to be distressed or upset, then it would be better for him to abstain from meat. The important principle was to choose the better (consider others) in preference to insisting on personal rights (eating meat), a principle that holds across a wide range of issues, even in the present day.

So far we have considered the differences between Jewish and Gentile believers during the book of Acts. But what happened at the end of Acts and afterwards?

Chapter 12

The Place of the Law in the post-Acts Period

The general pattern of the Acts Period is that a number of Jews came to believe that Jesus was the Messiah, the Son of God and their Saviour, but many did not. The leadership, as they were when Christ was on earth, were especially hardened. We see Peter and John running into difficulties with the authorities in Acts 4:1-21 and again in Acts 5:17-40. Paul frequently had problems with the Jewish leadership in the synagogues where he preached. Often they would get the civil authorities on their side (Acts 14:5; 17:5-9; 18:12; 19:9).

When Paul reached Rome he called together the leaders of the Jews, and he tried to convince them about Jesus. Some believed and some did not (Acts 28:17, 23-25). Following this we read the last New Testament pronouncement of Isaiah's prophecy of judgment upon Israel.[7] Quoting from Isaiah 6:9-10, Paul stated:

> "Go to this people and say, 'You will be ever hearing but never understanding; you will be ever seeing but never perceiving.' For this people's heart has become calloused; they hardly hear with their ears, and they have closed their eyes. Otherwise they might see with their eyes, hear with their ears, understand with their hearts and turn, and I would heal them." (Acts 28:26-27)

To Isaiah's prophecy Paul adds his own judgment on the nation:

> "Therefore I want you to know that God's salvation has been sent to the Gentiles, and they will listen!" (Acts 28:28)

---

[7] See *The Most Quoted Old Testament Prophecy* by Michael Penny, available from The Open Bible Trust

Shortly after Isaiah's original pronouncement, Judah was conquered by Nebuchadnezzar. He destroyed Jerusalem and the temple and scattered the Jews over his kingdom. Within about seven years of Paul citing this prophecy, the Romans destroyed Jerusalem and the temple, and scattered the people all over their empire.

The Jewish leaders had rejected Christ for over three years. They also rejected the teaching of the Apostles for over thirty years. This situation could not go on. The Jewish leadership grew increasingly hostile, and Josephus records a significant event, which took place about the same time as Paul was speaking to the leaders of the Jews in Rome. In Josephus: *Antiquities of the Jews*: 20,9,1 we read:

> The high priest, Ananus the Younger, a Sadducee ... Assembled the Sanhedrin of the judges and had brought before them the brother of Jesus, who was called Christ, whose name was James and some others; and when he had formed an accusation against them as breakers of the law, he delivered them to be stoned.

And so James, the brother of Jesus, and other Christian leaders in Jerusalem, were stoned to death on the orders of the high priest and Sanhedrin. After nearly 35 years of continual opposition enough was enough. Israel lost their privileged position as a special nation before God and fell under His judgment. His salvation would now go to the Gentiles.

What difference did this make to the will of God, especially for the Jewish Christians?

The Law of Moses abolished!

Following this last pronouncement of Isaiah's judgmental prophecy upon Israel, Paul wrote seven letters: Ephesians, Philippians, Colossians, 1 & 2 Timothy, Titus, and Philemon. The tone and flavour of these is somewhat different from his earlier letters, and from the letters of James, Peter, John and Jude. The following are two significant passages:

Ephesians 2:14-16	Colossians 2:13-17
For he himself is our peace, who has made the two one and has destroyed the barrier, the dividing wall of hostility, by abolishing in his flesh the law with its commandments and regulations. His purpose was to create in himself one new man out of the two, thus making peace, and in this one body to reconcile both of them to God through the cross, by which he put to death their hostility.	God made you alive with Christ. He forgave us all our sins, having cancelled the written code, with its regulations, that was against us and that stood opposed to us; he took it away, nailing it to the cross.... Therefore do not let anyone judge you by what you eat or drink, or with regard to a religious festival, a New Moon celebration or a Sabbath day. These are a shadow of the things that were to come; the reality, however, is found in Christ.

In these two passages we read that the Law of Moses, with its commandments and ordinances, had been abolished. The written code had been cancelled and taken away. Therefore the Jewish Christians need no longer worry about keeping the Sabbath day. The Gentile Christians of the Acts Period did not keep the Sabbath. Now the Jewish Christians were freed from the Sabbath laws.

Neither need they worry about what they ate. The Jewish Christians could now eat pork or duck, and many other such foods, and the Gentiles did not have to worry about eating the meat of strangled animals (Acts 15:20). Things had changed.

The focus of the Acts period was the people of Israel. God did everything possible to encourage them to believe in Jesus, but because of their obstinacy they became blind and deaf: blind to the significance of the miracles they saw, and deaf to what the Apostles taught (Acts 28:26-27). The Christian Jew was no longer caught in the dilemma of witnessing to the non-Christian Jew and having fellowship with the Christian Gentile. The focus was now on the Gentiles, and God brought the Christian Jew and Christian Gentile together. He made them one, and a major aspect of that bringing together of Jews and Gentiles into one new man was the freeing of the Christian Jew from the need to follow the Mosaic Law. Thus circumcision was no longer required.

> In him [Christ] you were also circumcised, in the putting off of the sinful nature, not with a circumcision done by the hands of men but with the circumcision done by Christ. (Colossians 2:11)

Physical circumcision, which had been done by men, was replaced by spiritual circumcision, done by Christ; the sinful nature had been cut off. Paul now described

> Physical circumcision, which had been done by men, was replaced by spiritual circumcision, done by Christ.

circumcision as "mutilation of the flesh" (Philippians 3:2).

> Watch out for those dogs, those men who do evil, those mutilators of the flesh. For it is we who are the circumcision, we who worship by the Spirit of God, who glory in Christ Jesus, and who put no confidence in the flesh. (Philippians 3:2-3)

The Law Abolished ... at the end of Acts

There are some Christians who believe that the Law of Moses was abolished *at* the Cross and thus Paul, James, and the Jewish Christians of the Acts Period were wrong to continue in their observance of the Law. It is always dangerous if we have to blame the Apostles to support our own theology. The likelihood is that the Apostles were right, and we are wrong.

It would seem that one reason for the incorrect view that the Law was abolished *at* the Cross is a misunderstanding of two passages.

> For he himself is our peace, who has made the two one and has destroyed the barrier, the dividing wall of hostility, by

abolishing *in his flesh* the law with its commandments and regulations. (Ephesians 2:14-15)

He forgave us all our sins, having cancelled the written code, with its regulations, that was against us and that stood opposed to us; he took it away, *nailing it to the cross.* (Colossians 2:13-14)

Here we read that the written code was *nailed to the cross*, that the Law was abolished *in his flesh*. In other words the Law was abolished *by* the cross. This is absolutely correct. When our Lord died for the sins of the world, He fulfilled the sacrificial offerings of the Law and much more. Hence from then on there was no need for the Jews to continue in their observance of the Law, but God did not tell them at that time to stop keeping the Law. So, although the Law was abolished in principle at the cross, it was not in practice and, if we stop to think, we can understand why.

Following Christ's death, resurrection and ascension there appears to be relatively few Jewish Christians; 120 gathered in Jerusalem, but one suspects that there were more than this (Acts 1:15). If the Lord had told them they no longer needed to observe the Law of Moses, and if they had given up Sabbath observance and circumcision, they would rapidly have been rejected by the rest of Judaism. They would not have been listened to, and their message would have been rejected. As it was they did not give up the Law, and they *were* listened to. Their message was accepted and three thousand were saved on the Day of Pentecost, and the number of men rose to five thousand a little while later (Acts 2:41; 4:4). And in Acts 21:20 James could say, "You see, brother, how many thousands of Jews have believed."

But it was not just for pragmatic reasons that Christian Jews during the Acts period were zealous for the Law. As we have noted, the message preached during Acts was a continuation of the

> Israel was still at the forefront of God's purposes and the overriding aim of the apostles' ministry was to turn the hearts of Israel to their Messiah.

message preached in the Gospels – it was to the Jew first. Israel was still at the forefront of God's purposes and the over-riding aim of the apostles' ministry was to turn the hearts of Israel to their Messiah. It would have been inappropriate to abandon the observances and practices that had been at the centre of Israel's religious life for centuries. In Matthew 5:17-18 the Lord Jesus Christ said:

> Do not think that I have come to abolish the Law or the Prophets; I have not come to abolish them but to fulfill them. I tell you the truth, until heaven and earth disappear, not the smallest letter, not the least stroke of a pen, will by any means disappear from the Law until everything is accomplished.

The Lord fulfilled the Law and the Prophets, and everything was accomplished by Him on the Cross. Thus He could have abolished the Law anytime after Calvary, but He did not do so until Israel had hardened their hearts, shut their eyes, and closed their ears (Acts 28:26-27). We do not read about the Law being abolished until we come to Ephesians and Colossians, both written during Paul's two year imprisonment in Rome mentioned in Acts 28:30.

In summary...

The Jewish leadership, in particular, opposed the revelation that Jesus was Israel's Messiah and, following the indecision of the leaders of the Jewish community in Rome, Paul quoted Isaiah's prophecy of judgment on Israel for a final time. Within a few short years Jerusalem was destroyed and the nation was scattered.

However, in Ephesians and Colossians, written after his condemnation of Israel in Acts 28, Paul revealed that the Law of Moses had been abolished. This abolition had been accomplished by the work of Christ on the cross, but the fact was not revealed until after the revelation of God's purposes to bring Jewish and Gentile believers together into one new man.

God's will for all Christians, whether they were Jews or Gentiles, was now the same. So what effect did this abolishment of the Law have on the will of God for Christians living in the post-Acts period?

Chapter 13
The Will of God for Christians in the post-Acts Period

Paul wrote seven letters after the end of the Acts period – Ephesians, Philippians, Colossians, 1 and 2 Timothy, Titus, and Philemon. Something significant had happened at the end of Acts. Because of the nation's hardness of heart, Israel had lost its

> Because of the nation's hardness of heart, Israel had lost its prime position and God's salvation was to be sent to the Gentiles.

prime position and God's salvation was to be sent to the Gentiles (Acts 28:25-28). The implication of this was that there would eventually be fewer Jewish and more Gentile Christians. In Colossians 4:10-11 Paul names just three Jewish Christians and states "These are the *only* Jews among my fellow workers." During Acts the Jewish Christians held first place, and were the teachers and leaders. They had the advantage because they had the Scriptures (Romans 3:1-2) and so could teach the Gentiles. However, if their numbers were diminishing the Gentiles would need teaching on how they should live in accordance with the will of God and so please Him. Therefore Paul wrote a great deal in these epistles on how post-Acts Christians should live.

Understanding the Lord's will – the worthy walk

In the *King James Version* (and the *New King James Version*), in Ephesians, Philippians and Colossians, Paul uses the expression 'walk' a number of times (translated as 'live' in the *NIV*). For example we read:

> Be very careful, then, how you live (walk circumspectly – *KJV*) - not as unwise but as wise, making the most of every opportunity, because the days are evil. Therefore do not be foolish, but understand what the Lord's will is. (Ephesians 5:15-17)

Here we have a clear indication that understanding the Lord's will results in a careful and wise life (walk). Ephesians, Philippians and Colossians teach us that we should live in a way that is worthy of the Lord, the Gospel and our calling. What does this entail?

In Colossians 1:9, Paul prays that the Christians will be filled with the knowledge of God's will through all spiritual wisdom and understanding. For what purpose? Paul goes on to explain:

> And we pray this in order that you may live a life [walk] worthy of the Lord and may please him in every way: bearing fruit in every good work, growing in the knowledge of God. (Colossians 1:10)

This worthy walk, which is pleasing to God, shows itself in two ways:

By growing in the knowledge of God

Here, the word translated 'knowledge' is the Greek *epignosis* which means either a deeper knowledge or acknowledgement. Here it probably takes the latter sense as Paul wanted them not only to improve their knowledge of God, but also to increase in their acknowledgement of Him and His ways in their lives.

As our understanding of the Lord, and of His perspective on situations grows, and as we put that knowledge into practice, we will see that His ways are right. Paul wanted the Romans to do just this, to test God's will and prove it to be the best (Romans 12:2). If we do this we are more likely to make not only good decisions, but the best. This idea also comes through in Paul's prayer for the Philippians.

> And this is my prayer: that your love may abound more and more in knowledge and depth of insight, so that you may be able to discern what is *best* and may be pure and blameless until the day of Christ, filled with the fruit of righteousness that comes through Jesus Christ – to the glory and praise of God. (Philippians 1:9-11)

We can see this principle being applied in Romans 14, which we considered earlier: for Gentile Christians to exercise their freedom to eat any kind of meat was *good* but if this would cause another Christian to stumble it was *best* to abstain.

Ephesians chapters 1-3 and Colossians chapters 1-2 are often described as the doctrinal sections of these epistles and the remaining chapters as the practical sections, dealing with different aspects of the worthy walk. Why does Paul present the doctrine first? It is essential that we first know our standing before Him: forgiven and very much loved. We also need to understand something of God's purposes for the universe and our place in these purposes. Only then can we gain a right perspective on our lives and realise that the conduct God asks of us comes from His knowing what is best, for both the individual and for society at large.

His desire is for us to live in a way that is appropriate for someone who is united with Christ. In other words it is a lifestyle that is "worthy" of who we are in Him. This is why it is so important to understand Christian doctrine. Our knowledge of God develops through the work of the Holy Spirit with whom we are sealed (Ephesians 1:13), as we pray to the Lord, meditate on His truth and put it into practice.

A deeper knowledge of God should also protect us from attack. In Ephesians 6, Paul urged the Christians to stand their ground and "put on" the full armour of God (which suggests it is

> Paul's desire is for us to live in a way that is appropriate for someone who is united with Christ.

possible for believers not to wear it!). The elements of this armour relate to our understanding of God and His ways – committed to truth, covered by His righteousness, confident in the gospel of peace, protected by the shield of faith and able to wield the word of God like a sword. It is not only the theoretical knowledge of these elements that is required. We need to 'wear' them on a daily basis. If we do not grow in our acknowledgement of Him, we are in danger of falling to Satan's attacks.

Paul uses a different metaphor in Colossians to show how we can be strengthened:

So then, just as you received Christ Jesus as Lord, continue to live [walk] in him, rooted and built up in him, strengthened in the faith as you were taught, and overflowing with thankfulness. (Colossians 2:6-7)

Walking in Christ will result in a strengthened faith and an overflowing thankfulness which banishes grumbling and discontentment. In Philippians 2:14-16 Paul wrote that they were to "do everything without complaining or arguing" and, if they did so, they would appear as blameless and pure children of God, and shine like stars in a crooked and depraved generation.

Be wise in the way you act [walk] toward outsiders; make the most of every opportunity. Let your conversation be always full of grace, seasoned with salt, so that you may know how to answer everyone. (Colossians 4:5-6)

This is similar to what Paul wrote to the Ephesians (5:15-17). Many watch us Christians and are quick to criticise what we do, what we say, and even the way in which we say it. Thus we need to be careful in our conversation; not only should there be no complaining and arguing, but all that we say should be full of grace; not only should we speak the truth, but we should always speak the truth 'in love' (Ephesians 4:15).

By bearing fruit in every good work

However, the worthy walk in Colossians 1:10 also results in good works, which follow on from our acknowledgement of Him.
Ephesians also speaks of "good works."

For we are God's workmanship, created in Christ Jesus to do good works, which God prepared in advance for us to do. (that we should walk in them – *KJV*). (Ephesians 2:10)

Some wonder what are the good works that God has prepared in advance for us to 'walk' in? The answer is best supplied by Scripture and later in Ephesians Paul lists a number of good works:

> As a prisoner for the Lord, then, I urge you to live a life worthy [walk worthy] of the calling you have received. Be completely humble and gentle; be patient, bearing with one another in love. Make every effort to keep the unity of the Spirit through the bond of peace. (Ephesians 4:1-3)

The first characteristics of this worthy walk are to:

- be completely humble and gentle;
- be patient;
- bear with one another in love.

And all these are necessary when dealing with other Christians if we are to guard the unity of the Spirit by living peacefully with one another.

The second aspect of the worthy walk that Paul wrote about was the need for godly thinking:

> So I tell you this, and insist on it in the Lord, that you must no longer live [walk] as the Gentiles do, in the futility of their *thinking*. They are darkened in their understanding and separated from the life of God because of the ignorance that is in them due to the hardening of their hearts. Having lost all sensitivity, they have given themselves over to sensuality so as to indulge in every kind of impurity, with a continual lust for more. (Ephesians 4:17-19)

The Greco-Roman world of that time was not too dissimilar to our own. Their trust in their high intellectual status had led them away from God and resulted in a decline in personal morality, with extreme sexual permissiveness and alcohol abuse being common. The Christians were not to live like that. Those who did, lived stupidly, not realising or caring what they were doing to their own bodies. Such a darkened understanding of life separated them from God and led to moral decline. Paul wanted the Christians to be 'imitators of God', but how could they do that?

> Be imitators of God, therefore, as dearly loved children and live a life of love [walk in love], just as Christ loved us and gave himself up for us as a fragrant offering and sacrifice to God. (Ephesians 5:1-2)

So to be an imitator of God they needed to 'live a life of love', that *agape* self-sacrificing love that puts the needs of others before the needs of self. That is the love Christ has for us; the love which led Him to give himself up for us and which He wants us to have for one another.

> For you were once darkness, but now you are light in the Lord. Live [walk] as children of light (for the fruit of the light consists in all goodness, righteousness and truth) and find out what pleases the Lord. Have nothing to do with the fruitless deeds of darkness, but rather expose them. (Ephesians 5:8-11)

At one time these Gentile Christians walked in darkness, which was a futile way to live. There is no lasting pleasure, satisfaction or contentment in such a lifestyle, either for the person himself, or for anyone else. In contrast, believers are children of light, and so they should walk in the light, and walking in the light, by contrast, produces an abundance of fruit: goodness, righteousness and truth.

What does that mean in practical terms? Paul has already explained earlier in Ephesians:

> Therefore each of you must put off falsehood and speak truthfully to his neighbour, for we are all members of one body. "In your anger do not sin": Do not let the sun go down while you are still angry, and do not give the devil a foothold. (4:25-27)

He who has been stealing must steal no longer, but must work, doing something useful with his own hands, that he may have something to share with those in need. (4:28)

Do not let any unwholesome talk come out of your mouths, but only what is helpful for building others up according to their needs, that it may benefit those who listen. And do not grieve the Holy Spirit of God, with whom you were sealed for the day of redemption. (4:29-30)

Get rid of all bitterness, rage and anger, brawling and slander, along with every form of malice. Be kind and compassionate to one another, forgiving each other, just as in Christ God forgave you. (4:31-32)

But among you there must not be even a hint of sexual immorality, or of any kind of impurity, or of greed, because these are improper for God's holy people. Nor should there be obscenity, foolish talk or coarse joking, which are out of place, but rather thanksgiving. (5:3-4)

The worthy walk impacts on the way we speak – committed to the truth and to edifying rather than unwholesome conversation; it affects the attitudes we have – kindness, compassion and forgiveness rather than bitterness and anger, and it governs what we do – avoiding sexual immorality and working rather than stealing.

In Colossians 3:5-17 Paul gave similar instructions on what they should not do (practices relating to their sinful, earthly nature) followed by a list of what they should do (the good fruit and good works wanted by God). First they were told to put to death:

> The worthy walk impacts on the way we speak; it affects the attitudes we have; it governs what we do.

- sexual immorality, impurity, lust, evil desires and greed.

Next they were told to get rid of such practices as:

- anger, rage, malice, slander, filthy language and lying.

Then they were told to clothe themselves with:

- compassion, kindness, humility, gentleness and patience.

And finally they were told to:

- Forgive as the Lord forgave them, put on love, let the peace of Christ rule in their hearts and be thankful.

Good examples and bad

> Only let us live [walk] up to what we have already attained. Join with others in following my example, brothers, and take note of those who live [walk] according to the pattern we gave you. For, as I have often told you before and now say again even with tears, many live [walk] as enemies of the cross of Christ. (Philippians 3:16-18)

The sad situation in Philippi was that some of the Christians had slipped back into old ways, and were living as though they were not Christians. Paul exhorted them to follow his example and the example of other Christians who lived up to the Christ-like pattern.

The new Gentile Christians of that time, like new Christians today, needed so much guidance and advice if they were to know the will of God, follow it and put it into practice, and so please Him. The danger was always there, that they would lose sight of their identity in Christ and revert back to their old pagan habits. Paul encouraged them by suggesting that they look to mature believers who were walking in a worthy way and follow their lead.

They, like Christians today, were a minority group in an unsympathetic society. They needed to be careful how they lived their lives in public and needed to make the most of every opportunity. They were not to be foolish in what they did. They needed to get to know and understand what the Lord's will was for them, i.e. how they should run their lives.

It is an extremely high standard that is set before us. Our Heavenly Father wants us to be increasingly like the Lord Jesus Christ. How can we hope to come close to such a standard? At the start of the third chapter of Colossians Paul gave some good advice to his readers. As a fundamental principle, they should follow the mind-set that is appropriate for someone who has been brought into the Lord's family:

> Since, then, you have been raised with Christ, set your hearts on things above, where Christ is seated at the right hand of God. Set your minds on things above, not on earthly things. (Colossians 3:1-2)

| As a fundamental principle, they should follow the mind-set that is appropriate for someone who has been brought into the Lord's family. |

So, when problems and difficulties, trials and temptations come on this earth, look away from them to things above, to where Christ is seated at the right hand of God in the heavenly realms, because that is where we shall be in eternity (Ephesians 2:6-7). Philippians also talks of those who have their minds on 'earthly things' but Paul told them "our citizenship is in heaven" (Philippians 3:19-20). And the advice he gave the Philippians was not dissimilar.

> Finally, brothers, whatever is true, whatever is noble, whatever is right, whatever is pure, whatever is lovely, whatever is admirable—if anything is excellent or praiseworthy—think about such things. Whatever you have learned or received or heard from me, or seen in me—put it into practice. And the God of peace will be with you. (Philippians 4:8-9)

In Philippians 1:27-28 Paul speaks of the worthy life in terms of unity within the fellowship.

Whatever happens, conduct yourselves in a manner worthy of the gospel of Christ. Then, when I come and see you or only hear about you in my absence, I will know that you stand firm in one spirit, contending as one man for the faith of the gospel without being frightened in any way by those who oppose you.

The picture here is of Christian believers being united in proclaiming the gospel and boldly facing opposition together. In order for a Christian group to be united, the relationships between its members need to be right.

Right Relationships

Right relationships are at the core of God's will for His people. The instructions for the worthy walk are paramount for right relationships between believers, and in these last letters of Paul there is a great deal of teaching on relationships: relationships between:

- God and People
- Husbands and Wives
- Children and Parents
- Slaves and Masters
- Christians and Christians
- Churches and Leaders

God and People

It is clear that people are saved by grace through faith (Ephesians 2:8) and earlier Paul had written:

And you also were included in Christ when you heard the word of truth, the gospel of your salvation. Having believed, you were marked in him with a seal, the promised Holy Spirit, who is a deposit guaranteeing our inheritance until the redemption of those who are God's possession—to the praise of his glory. (Ephesians 1:13-14)

This gospel of salvation is that Christ died for our sins and rose again on the third day, and by believing we are justified, or reckoned righteous. Through Christ we have access to the Father by the Spirit (Ephesians 2:18) and believers in the gospel of salvation in Christ are sealed with the Spirit for the day of redemption (Ephesians 4:30).

> Christ is going to present the whole church to himself as a radiant church, without stain or wrinkle, or any other blemish, but holy and blameless.

In Christ we are blessed with every spiritual blessing (Ephesians 1:3) and in the Father's eyes believers are "holy and blameless" and free from accusation (Ephesians 1:4; Colossians 1:22). Christ is going to present the whole church to himself as a radiant church, without stain or wrinkle, or any other blemish, but holy and blameless (Ephesians 5:25-27). So complete and perfect is the salvation that Christ accomplished.

That is the relationship that God, in Christ, has with us. It is a Father / child relationship; one of love and looking at His children through rose-coloured spectacles, forgiving and forgetting their misdemeanours. So how should believers relate to Him? As a child who is dependent upon his Father; a child who appreciates what his Father has done for him, who loves his Father and who wants to please Him. So what pleases our heavenly Father? The answer to that question lies, in general, in the Bible. However, for us Gentiles living in the post-Acts Period, it lies more specifically in the last seven letters of Paul and these are the ones we are considering in this chapter.

> So complete and perfect is the salvation that Christ accomplished.

Husbands and Wives

The essential unit for any society is the family, and a successful family revolves around the parents, the husband and wife. Paul has two sections dealing with husbands and wives in these letters.

In Ephesians 5:22-24 and Colossians 3:18 wives are told simply to 'submit' to their own husbands. The reason given is that the husband is 'head' of the wife. However, we must not misunderstand the symbolism behind the word 'head'. Today we tend to look upon the 'head' as that part of our anatomy which controls the body. However, in New Testament times it was seen as that part of the body which supplied all the needs of the body. It is through the head that we take in food, drink and air, and we see, hear and smell with parts of the head.

Christ is head of the church, His body, but He is not an authoritarian, controlling head. He is the One who supplies all the needs of the church. He is the One who was delivered over to death for our sins and was raised to life for our justification (Romans 4:25). And of Him Paul wrote:

> And my God will meet all your **needs** according to his glorious riches in Christ Jesus. (Philippians 4:19)

Thus Paul wrote that wives were to submit to their husbands because the husband supplied all the needs of the family.

In the Greco-Roman world of that day there was much divorce and little true love between many husbands and wives. Paul left Titus in charge of the church in Crete, and gave him much advice about which problems to tackle and what to teach. In Titus 2:2-5 we read:

> Teach the older men to be temperate, worthy of respect, self-controlled, and sound in faith, in love and in endurance. Likewise, teach the older women to be reverent in the way they live, not to be slanderers or addicted to much wine, but to teach what is good. Then they can train the younger women to love their husbands and children, to be self-controlled and pure, to be busy at home, to be kind, and to be subject to their husbands, so that no-one will malign the word of God.

It may sound strange to us that younger women would need to be *trained* to love their husbands. However, these Gentile Christian women may have had little understanding of the self-sacrificing *agape* love of the Bible. Although *agape* is a Greek word it is hardly found in secular Greek and Archbishop Trench said that it is a word 'born within the bosom of revealed religion'. So high and holy was this love that the Greeks seldom used the word; they knew that they could not live up to it, and neither could Christians, were it not for the help of the indwelling Holy Spirit and His power (Ephesians 3:16-19). The young Greek Christian women on Crete needed to be taught what true love was.

> *agape* is a word that is hardly found in secular Greek and Archbishop Trench said that it is a word 'born within the bosom of revealed religion'

As for husbands: Colossians 3:19 simply states:

Husbands, love your wives and do not be harsh with them.

The husband may supply all the needs of his wife, and she may well be subject to him and submit to him, but he did not own her. She was not a possession, a thing; she was a person with feelings. Thus a harsh authoritarian attitude was unfitting.

Ephesians, however, has much more to say to the husband, but from a positive perspective. Three times Paul tells husbands to love their wives, and each time describes that love a little differently. In Ephesians 5:25-33 we read:

1. Husbands, love your wives, just as Christ loved the church and gave himself up for it[8]. (5:25)
2. Husbands ought to love their wives as their own bodies (5:28)
3. A husband must love his wife as he loves himself. (5:33)

First of all we have a straight statement: Husbands, love your wives, just as Christ loved the church and gave himself up for it.

---

[8] In Ephesians 5:25 the *KJV* refers to the church as 'it', which is more accurate than the 'her' of the *NIV*. The Greek word for 'church' is **not** feminine and the church of Ephesians is the body of Christ.

Next we have a more forceful statement: Husbands *ought* to love their wives as their own bodies. And finally, we have a direct command: a husband *must* love his wife as he loves himself.

A man supplying the needs of his wife and family, and a wife respecting and submitting to her husband, that is the secret of a happy marriage. A mutually self-sacrificing love in which each puts the worries and wants of the other before themselves - that is what children need to see in their parents.

Children and Parents

Colossians 3:20 tells children to "obey your parents in everything, for this pleases the Lord", and in Ephesians 6:1-3 we have the same command. However, Paul reminds his readers that this was such an important command for an orderly society that in the Law of Moses it was the first commandment God gave which carried with it a promise for the people of Israel (see Deuteronomy 5:16).

| Fathers, do not exasperate your children; instead, bring them up in the training and instruction of the Lord. (Ephesians 6:4) | Fathers, do not embitter your children, or they will become discouraged. (Colossians 3:21) |

Just as the men, as husbands, were told not to be harsh towards their wives but to love them, so the men, as fathers, were told not to annoy and frustrate their children. If they did so, they might discourage them. However, it was the father's responsibility to ensure that his children were instructed in the ways of the Lord.

This was especially the case for those men who were being considered for positions of responsibility in the church. For example: an overseer "must manage his own family well and see that ... his children obey him with proper respect" (1 Timothy 3:4) and a deacon "must manage his children and his household well" (1 Timothy 3:12). An elder must be "a man whose children believe and are not open to the charge of being wild and disobedient" (Titus 1:6).

Slaves and Masters

There are a number of passages addressed to the Christian slaves of that era, much of which may be applicable to employees of today.

Slaves, obey your earthly masters with respect and fear, and with sincerity of heart, just as you would obey Christ. Obey them not only to win their favour when their eye is on you, but like slaves of Christ, doing the will of God from your heart. Serve wholeheartedly, as if you were serving the Lord, not men, because you know that the Lord will reward everyone for whatever good he does, whether he is slave or free. (Ephesians 6:5-8)	Slaves, obey your earthly masters in everything; and do it, not only when their eye is on you and to win their favour, but with sincerity of heart and reverence for the Lord. Whatever you do, work at it with all your heart, as working for the Lord, not for men, since you know that you will receive an inheritance from the Lord as a reward. It is the Lord Christ you are serving. Anyone who does wrong will be repaid for his wrong, and there is no favouritism. (Coloss. 3:22-25)

Christianity, at that time, was not in a position to change the laws of the land. It could not! There was no democracy, just the Roman Empire so … what was best for the slaves, and what was most likely to spread the Christian message? It was to obey and respect, even if the master wasn't looking. Obey and respect them as they would Christ. And Paul gave similar advice to Timothy and Titus as to what they should teach the slaves (1Timothy 6:1-2; Titus 2:9-10).

As for the Christian masters, what were they to do? Free the slaves? Paul did not say that. In general terms his teaching was:

And masters, treat your slaves in the same way. Do not threaten them, since you know that he who is both their Master and yours is in heaven, and there is no favouritism with him. (Ephesians 6:9)	Masters, provide your slaves with what is right and fair, because you know that you also have a Master in heaven. (Colossians 4:1)

Just as men who were husbands were told not to be harsh towards their wives, and men who were fathers were told not to exasperate their children, men who were masters were told not to threaten their slaves, but instead to deal justly with them. However, to one slave master he gave some very different advice as to how he should treat his slave. He told Philemon to receive back the runaway slave Onesimus not as a slave "but better than a slave, as a dear brother" and Philemon was to welcome him as he would welcome Paul (Philemon 16-17). Whether or not Philemon did welcome Onesimus as a 'brother' we do not know, but this was tantamount to giving Onesimus his freedom.

Christians and Christians

Relationships between Christians are critical. How they treat one another is of great importance. In fact our Lord Jesus Christ told His disciples:

> "A new command I give you: Love one another. As I have loved you, so you must love one another. By this all men will know that you are my disciples, if you love one another." (John 13:34-35)

Thus, how Christians relate to one another either enhances the Christian witness or detracts from it. Paul wrote a number of commands as to how Christians should treat one another and these have been considered in the previous section. The overriding principle is that they should be likeminded, having the same attitude as the Lord Jesus Christ, who considered the interests of others to be more important than His own (Philippians 2:1-5). So, for example, in Ephesians we read:

- Be completely humble and gentle; be patient, bearing with one another in love. (4:2)
- Be kind and compassionate to one another, forgiving each other, just as in Christ God forgave you. (4:32)

- Speak to one another with psalms, hymns and spiritual songs. (5:19)
- Submit to one another out of reverence for Christ. (5:21)

In Colossians Paul wrote:

- Do not lie to each other, since you have taken off your old self with its practices. (3:9)
- Bear with each other and forgive whatever grievances you may have against one another. Forgive as the Lord forgave you. (3:13)
- Let the word of Christ dwell in you richly as you teach and admonish one another with all wisdom, and as you sing psalms, hymns and spiritual songs with gratitude in your hearts to God. (3:16)

Christians should therefore be loving and forgiving towards one another; they should display humility and patience. There should be no lies and no unwholesome talk. Rather the conversation should be spiritual, based on psalms, hymns and spiritual songs, and the Word of Christ, so that it will build others up.

> Christians should be loving and forgiving towards one another; they should display humility and patience.

Churches and Leaders

During the Gospels Christ Himself chose those who were to be the leaders. In fact this continued during the Acts period and even in Ephesians we read that it was He who gave "some to be apostles, some to be prophets, some to be evangelists, and some to be pastors and teachers" and that these were to be given until those people reached a unity in the faith (Ephesians 4:11-13). But what happened when they did reach that unity? Earlier Paul had said that prophecies and various others gifts would cease (1 Corinthians 13:8-10).

During the Acts Period we had overseers, (*episkopos*; translated 'bishops' in some versions) and these had been appointed by the Holy Spirit (Acts 20:28). However, with the cessation of the Apostles and prophets, and other Christ and Holy Spirit appointees, what was going to happen? Men were going to make the appointments, as they do today. We read in Timothy about the type of person he should appoint as an overseer and a deacon (*diakonos*), and Titus is given similar information about elders (*presbuteros*).

> Overseers: see 1 Timothy 3:1-7.
> Deacons: see 1 Timothy 3:8-13.
> Elders: see Titus 1:5-9.

From these we can see that the man's character must be exemplary. Then, with respect to how such leaders relate to others in the church, we see that they must be temperate and self-controlled, neither violent nor quarrelsome, and must be able to teach (1 Timothy 3:1-7). They must not be overbearing or quick tempered, but rather self-controlled and hospitable and they must be able to encourage others (Titus 1:5-9). In 2 Timothy 2:24-25 we read:

> The Lord's servant must not quarrel; instead, he must be kind to everyone, able to teach, not resentful. Those who oppose him he must gently instruct, in the hope that God will grant them repentance leading them to a knowledge of the truth.

But how should the church treat its leaders? As we have just read, the Christian leader, unfortunately, is likely to have opposition and sometimes opponents do not stick to the argument, but look to attack the character. This may be why Paul wrote that they should not entertain an accusation against an elder unless it is brought by two or three witnesses (1 Timothy 5:19).

The church in Philippi was led by overseers and deacons (Philippians 1:1) and we know that this church was generous with gifts to Paul. In fact Paul wrote that all churches should be generous towards their leaders, especially their teachers, as he stated in 1 Timothy 5:17-18:

The elders who direct the affairs of the church well are worthy of double honour, especially those whose work is preaching and teaching. For the Scripture says, "Do not muzzle the ox while it is treading out the grain," and "The worker deserves his wages."

In summary...

In our day and age the Lord calls us to live a life that is worthy of Him, worthy of the Gospel and worthy of our calling. That, in essence, is His will for us. Our lifestyle follows on from our understanding of God's character and purposes and the fact that we are predestined to be adopted as His sons through Christ (Ephesians 1:5). We must behave appropriately as His children and bear fruit in every good work. These fruits develop in our lives as the Lord works on us by His Spirit. As Paul said in Galatians:

> The fruit of the Spirit is love, joy, peace, patience, kindness, goodness, faithfulness, gentleness and self-control.
> (Galatians 5:22, 23)

That fruit will grow in every dimension of our lives – our attitudes, our thinking, our speech, our actions and, above all, in our relationships with one another and with those we meet on a daily basis.

This was the will of God for Christians living in the post-Acts Period, to whom Paul was writing. That is the period we live in and so this is the will of God for us who live in this current Age of Grace. It was so important for them to live like that if they were to stand firm, and it is important for us also.

However, we live nearly 2,000 years after these words were written. Our world is very different and new problems have arisen which are not covered in Scripture so we need to consider *the will of God for the 21st Century*. However, before doing that, we shall pull together what we have seen concerning the will of God throughout the Scriptures, paying particular attention to what God has required of Gentiles and what He wanted in the post-Acts Period, the one in which we live.

Chapter 14
The will of God in the Bible:
Summary and Conclusion

The progressive revelation of the will of God

It is clear from the Scriptures that the will of God was for His people to follow His commandments; the Lord said, "If you love me, you will obey what I command," (John 14:15). For the Jews of the Old Testament, Gospel Period and Acts Period this included observing the Law of Moses, but Christ wanted them to embrace the spirit of the Law in their hearts and extend the reach of love. For the first Christian Gentiles of the Acts Period the will of God was to live loving, caring and moral lives, and to observe the four rules of the Jerusalem council.

However, once we reach the post-Acts period we find the Law of Moses, circumcision, the Sabbath and dietary regulations had been abolished for the Christian Jew. Of course, it is worth noting that this was mainly to do with the ceremonial and ritualistic side of that Law. The moral issues, the love and the care the Law contained, were expanded by Christ, repeated in practical teaching contained in the letters written during the Acts period, and taught in those last letters Paul wrote in the post-Acts period. So, the will of God for Christians after the end of Acts right up to the present day is the same in that respect.

> The moral issues, the love and the care the Law contained, were expanded by Christ, repeated in the letters written during the Acts period, and taught in the last letters Paul wrote.

Changes in God's revelation of His will

It is important to recognise that there were changes over time, both in terms of the content of the Lord's revealed will and the ways in which He revealed it. We are not Jews living during Old Testament times, or when our Lord was on earth or during the Acts period. Thus we do not need to worry about keeping the Law of Moses.

In addition, some of the teachings our Lord gave to the Jews, or to the Twelve, when on earth, may not apply to us. For example, He told the Twelve that in the Kingdom they would sit on twelve thrones judging the twelve tribes of Israel (Matthew 19:28). Few today would see that as applying to them.

Similarly, He also told them that "I will do whatever you ask in my name … You may ask me for anything in my name, and I will do it" (John 14:13-14) [9]. If we try to apply that to ourselves and say it is 'truth for today' we are likely to be very disappointed.

This also applies to some of the teachings given during the Acts period. There we are told that the gospel of salvation is first for the Jew (Romans 1:16), but today we do not have to preach the gospel to Jews before we can preach it to Gentiles. We read, too, that salvation has come to the Gentiles to make Israel envious (Romans 11:11). That may have been the situation during the Acts period (see e.g. Acts 13:45), but it is not the case today.

We saw, in the Old Testament, and at the start of Acts, that certain aspects of the will of God were found by casting lots or by the use of the Urim and Thummim. This was often to do with finding a person, or selecting a leader. They were not used for making everyday decisions.

Also God spoke directly to a few important people, often leaders, and gave a few others visions or dreams. However, the ordinary people do not appear to have been instructed in this way. They were to follow what was taught in the Scriptures. In Israel, in Old Testament times, individuals might visit a priest for information from the Lord.

When Christ was on earth, He chose the people He wanted as Apostles. During the Acts, apart from the selection of Matthias at the start, it was the Holy Spirit who made the selection (Acts 20:28). However, after Acts the situation changed. The appointments of leaders were then made by people, and that is still the case today, with interview panels and so on. However, Paul gave guidance to Timothy and Titus about the type of people they should appoint; see 1 Timothy

---

[9] For a full treatment of these verses see pages 138 – 148 of *40 Problem Passages* by Michael Penny, available from The Open Bible Trust.

3:1-13 and Titus 1:5-9 as to the qualities needed for a Christian leader. Today we ignore that advice at our peril.

The will of God in the Bible

If we wish to find the Lord's will for today we need to look to the Scriptures. Succinctly, the will of God for us Christians today can be summed up in the words of Ephesians 4:1.

> As a prisoner for the Lord, then, I urge you to live a life worthy of the calling you have received.

The worthy walk is our response to the reality of our position in Christ. God asks us to recognise who we are in Him, and act accordingly. Our whole mindset has changed from when we were unbelievers. As Paul says in Colossians 3:1-4:

> Since, then, you have been raised with Christ, *set your hearts on things above*, where Christ is seated at the right hand of God. Set *your minds on things above*, not on earthly things. For you died, and your life is now hidden with Christ in God. When Christ, who is your life, appears, then you also will appear with him in glory.

The attitudes, actions and relationships that are characteristic of "things above" are explained in detail in Paul's seven letters written after the end of Acts - Ephesians, Philippians, Colossians, 1 & 2 Timothy, Titus and Philemon. It is therefore imperative that we do our utmost to follow the practical teaching in these epistles. When we study these and find out what it is, we should not be surprised to find that the moral

> The attitudes, actions and relationships that are characteristic of "things above" are explained in detail in Paul's seven letters written after the end of Acts.

and ethical teachings of the Mosaic Law, of the Prophets in the Old Testament, of our Saviour in the Gospels, of the Apostles during the

Acts Period, and of Paul's post-Acts Period letters, have very much in common.

The Scriptures contain God's revealed will for His people. The Scriptures are all we need to be equipped for doing good. As Paul says to Timothy:

> All Scripture is God-breathed and is useful for
> teaching,
> rebuking,
> correcting and
> training in righteousness,
> **so that**
> the man of God may be thoroughly equipped for every good work. (2 Timothy 3:16-17)

All we have and are is by the grace of God in Christ; what He is seeking from us is "every good work":

> For it is by grace that you have been saved, through faith – and this not from yourselves, it is the gift of God – not by works, so that no-one can boast. For we are God's workmanship, created in Christ Jesus to do good works, which God prepared in advance for us to do. (Ephesians 2:8-10)

So what are these good works which God has prepared in advance for us to do? Some think that God has a whole series of secret deeds that He has pre-planned for each individual to do, and each person has to struggle and strive to find out just what these are. However, it is extremely doubtful if this is what Paul meant or that God has a predetermined, detailed plan for each of us. (See the Appendix for a discussion of this issue).

In fact it is very easy to find out what these good works are. We do not need to pray for revelation or guidance. We do not need to seek the views of pastors or priests. We do not need to read philosophy or theology. All we need to do is *read the Bible* and pay particular attention to the moral and ethical teaching; the love and attitudes it advocates. These are the 'good works' God has prepared for us to do; this is His will for us. As we have said, we do not need to pray about these, although we will, naturally, pray about more personal matters and choices.

Strength for doing the will of God

However, although the Scriptures give us a clear view of what is expected of us, it sometimes can be hard for us to have the grace and strength (and courage) to do it. After all, it was the Apostle Paul, some 20 years or so after he became a Christian, who wrote:

> For I have the desire to do what is good, but I cannot carry it out. For what I do is not the good I want to do; no, the evil I do not want to do - this I keep on doing. (Romans 7:18-19)

He struggled at times, but he wrote to the Colossians, telling them to set their minds on things above, where they really belong and to live a life that is worthy of that calling (see Colossians 3:1-2).

That advice is good for us also. Setting our hearts and minds on things above will generate the right attitude of mind to ensure that we want to follow the will of God. However, we will need some help to do so and, thankfully, the Lord does not expect us to do it on our own. He has provided the *power* of His indwelling Holy Spirit.

I pray also that the eyes of your heart may be enlightened in order that you may know the hope to which he has called you, the riches of his

> Setting our hearts and minds on things above will generate the right attitude of mind to ensure that we want to follow the will of God.

glorious inheritance in the saints, and his incomparably great *power* for us who believe. That *power* is like the working of his mighty strength, which he exerted in Christ when he raised him from the dead and seated him at his right hand in the heavenly realms, far above all rule and authority, power and dominion, and every title that can be given, not only in the present age but also in the one to come. (Ephesians 1:18-21)

I pray that out of his glorious riches he may strengthen you with *power* through his Spirit in your inner being, so that Christ may dwell in your hearts through faith. And I pray that you, being rooted and established in love, may have *power*, together with all the saints, to grasp how wide and long and high and deep is the love of Christ, and to know this love that surpasses knowledge - that you may be filled to the measure of all the fullness of God. (Ephesians 3:16-19)

May that prayer become a reality in our experience.

Section 3

Implications and Possibilities for the 21st Century

Chapter 15
The 21ˢᵗ Century Environment:
A comparison with New Testament
times

The first two sections of the book have explored the will of God for His people and have noted that this is primarily communicated through the Scriptures. It is therefore important to know what the Bible has to say about how the Lord wants us to live and the sort of people He wants us to be. However, we stand almost 2,000 years after the last Scriptures were written. On the face of it our society and culture are very different from those of Paul and his contemporaries but in fact there are a number of similarities. The Greco-Roman world, like ours, laid great emphasis on sport and education, and it was also extremely sexually permissive.

Therefore, the principles laid down in Scripture in the first century are relevant to today and the Lord expects us, as Christians, to take and apply them to the 21ˢᵗ century. This means that we need to have an understanding of the nature of the world in which we live and the prevailing outlook. This will enable us to see how the Scriptures speak into our own situation.

Until fairly recently the basic assumptions of Christian morality were embedded in people's views of right and wrong, even if they were not explicitly articulated as a Christian worldview. That has now changed and very different

> The principles laid down in Scripture in the first century are relevant to today and the Lord expects us, as Christians, to take and apply them to the 21ˢᵗ century.

assumptions of morality are being absorbed into our thinking. Our post-modern society has largely rejected the idea of objective truth and replaced it with a more fluid, individualistic and flexible view of reality, with people's lifestyles and values being tailored to their personal preferences. This makes the Christian message of deliverance from judgment harder to accept, as there is a rejection of the concept of sin and absolute morality. There is also a deep suspicion of authority and authoritative statements. There are four main themes running through our society and this section of the book explores how following the will of God relates to these themes. They are:

- *Image: An obsession with the cult of personality:* Our television screens and social media are dominated by sportsmen and women, musicians, movie stars, celebrities and personalities some of whom are just "famous for being famous." Their hedonistic lifestyles and indiscretions are chewed over in detail and are a role model for many. This mindset makes the projected image of the person more important than the reality.

- *Self-fulfilment: A preoccupation with self and personal fulfilment*: The constant gratification of the self has become all-important. Many of our contemporaries use consumer spending as a way of defining their identity by linking themselves with particular brands and styles. This means continuous change as we re-invent ourselves and move on to the latest fashion. This outlook has been a major factor in the huge growth of the personal debt that is crippling our economy. Because the focus is on the self, and the image of the self, it also has a negative impact on the extent to which we accept any social responsibilities and commitment; the emphasis is more on our personal rights than our duties and has given rise to the expression 'personal wealth at the expense of public squalor.'

- *Unrestrained life choices: An acceptance of any lifestyle choice in others as long as it does not interfere or restrict us personally:* A writer in The Times recently summed up the current dominant ideology as "have a good time, don't judge, chill out." [10] As a result, any attempts to set moral boundaries are frowned upon. Sexual promiscuity, alcohol and drug abuse are tolerated and even celebrated as examples of our 'freedom.'

---

[10] Robert Crampton, *The Times*, 2 January 2012, pp34-35.

- *Atheism: The rise of aggressive, science-based atheism*: A hard atheism is being pushed through the media to the extent that all alternatives are dismissed or belittled. Science is believed to be the only discipline that is answering questions on the nature of man and the universe; scientific knowledge alone is real knowledge. Linked with this is a hostility towards Christianity in particular. Western media subject Christian belief to ridicule and abuse and there are forces dedicated to the removal of all Christian influence on society.

So our society is one that is hostile to the Christian message and not an easy environment for anyone who wants to live as God requires. Yet, when we examine the ground in which the first century church grew we discover that this was no less antagonistic to the message. In the Greco-Roman world high status was given to education and athletics. The gladiators and chariot racers of first century Rome were feted as heroes. One second century charioteer, Gaius Appuleius Diocles, is still regarded as the highest-paid sportsman of all time. At the same time personal morality was almost non-existent, with extreme sexual permissiveness and alcohol abuse being common.

The new 'sect' of the Christians was initially seen as a branch of Judaism. However, the Romans latterly saw Christianity as a threat to the status and personality cult of the emperor and persecution grew throughout the first century and beyond. In addition, many of the Christian virtues, such as humility, non-retaliation and prioritisation of the interests of others, were regarded as weaknesses in Roman culture and mocked. Christians following these aspects of the Lord's teaching in Roman colonies were despised by their fellow-citizens.

So there is a remarkable similarity between our world and that into which the fledgling church emerged. First and second century Christians faced opposition and pressures to conform that were similar to those we face. So the Scriptures that revealed God's will to the churches in Colosse, Philippi and Rome are no less relevant to

> First and second century Christians faced opposition and pressures to conform that were similar to those we face.

Christians today in London, New York and Paris.

Our society is a paradoxical one. On the one hand, post-modernism is characterised by a rejection of the 'big questions' – like the search for an overall purpose to life or a debate on the extent of our responsibility to society. Instead the emphasis is now on individuals defining ideas like 'truth,' 'fact', and 'reality' to suit themselves. They argue that something may be 'true' for me but not necessarily for someone else.

Yet, on the other hand, the big questions are everywhere:

- The financial crisis has seriously damaged the lives of millions. What can people hold on to when the economic model we have followed for so long has been shown up to be inadequate?

- The issue of global warming raises uncertainties and fears for the future. Regularly, scientific researchers announce the results of projections suggesting that the situation is worse than we thought. What does the future hold in relation to climate change?

- The search for significance in life. Science tells us that there is no purpose to our existence. We are a random collection of atoms brought together by time and chance. But is that all we are?

We are living at a critical time in history. Concern has been expressed by Christian and non-Christian writers alike that contemporary post-modern thinking will not be able to sustain civil and moral communities in the longer term.[11]

---

[11] Humanist writers Will and Ariel Durant, writing in 1977, warned that "We shall find it no easy task to mould a natural ethic strong enough to maintain moral restraint and social order without the support of supernatural consolations, hopes and fears." (*The Humanist*, February 1977) Recently, Alan de Botton, in his book, *Religion for Atheists*, (Hamish Hamilton, 2012) argues that secular society requires to establish its own institutions and practices to give space and support to our inner life without the "ideology and dogma" that follows on from religion It is extremely doubtful that this will be successful.

There is no doubt that, in the West, we are living in a post-Christian society, which is quite unsympathetic, even hostile in some cases, towards Christianity. How should Christians cope with this?

There is a danger that we will go to one of two extremes. There are those with a 'bunker' mentality: they stay in their churches and have as little contact with the world as possible. Others become chameleons, mirroring the morals and attitude of the world, not wanting to cause offence. Is either of these the will of God? Or is there a middle course somewhere between the two? If we are to be salt and light in the world, as the Lord instructed us (Matthew 5:13,14), neither of these extremes is appropriate. We must preserve our Christian distinctiveness but, at the same time, the Lord expects us to engage with a lost world to share His good news. This affects not only the words we say but also the kind of people we are. As Chick Yuill observes, "If we want people to listen to the good news we share, then we have to *be* good news."[12]

> We must preserve our Christian distinctiveness but, at the same time, the Lord expects us to engage with a lost world to share His good news.

So what is the will of God for us in the 21st century? And how do the various aspects of the will of God, as set out in the Scriptures, engage with the four themes of contemporary life identified above?

---

[12] Chick Yuill, *Moving in the right circles*, p133, Inter-Varsity Press, 2011.

In summary...

The world in which we are called to witness is very different from that of our parents and grandparents. The basic assumptions of Christian morality which used to underpin society are no longer in place and concepts of morality are much more fluid than they once were. The emphasis on individual freedom and the self-obsession of modern Western culture make it hard for the Christian message to take root.

However, the environment in which the young church grew in the first century was also hostile to the Christian message so the principles contained in Scripture are no less applicable to our own situation two thousand years later. Our world is a very needy one in both physical and spiritual terms and we are called to engage with the world without conforming ourselves to its values.

The previous section of the book considered Paul's teaching that Christians should live, or "walk" in a manner that is worthy of the Lord, His Gospel and His calling. Ephesians 5:15-17 shows the link between "walking" wisely and following the Lord's will. So how does He want us to apply the principles that He has set out in Scripture, in order that we may live worthy lives in the 21st century?

Chapter 16

Applying the Scriptures
to 21st Century Society

Colossians 1:10 sets out two aspects to living a life worthy of the Lord
and pleasing Him:

- Growing in the knowledge of God
  and
- Bearing fruit in every good work.

Growing in the knowledge of God: Doctrine and experience

As a starting point for the worthy walk, we must have an understanding
of God's purposes. The early sections of both Ephesians and Colossians
spell this out for us in some detail. In Ephesians 1:9-11 Paul explains
that God made known to us the mystery of His will, namely to bring all
things in heaven and on earth together under one head, even Christ
(verse 10). Ephesians 1 also explains our place in these purposes –
accomplished through the work of Christ (verses 5 and 6), secured
through believing the gospel of salvation (verse 13), and sealed by the
Holy Spirit as a deposit guaranteeing our inheritance (verses 13-14).
God has revealed the mystery of His will to us so that we may know the
hope to which He has called us (verse 18) – namely the riches of His
glorious inheritance in the saints. Colossians 1:12 echoes the same idea
– that God has qualified us to share in the inheritance of the saints in the
kingdom of light.

Why is it particularly important for us to grasp this truth in our
time? Firstly, because of the assurance it gives us. We live in a world
where nothing is certain. Even the existence of "factual" truth is
challenged and the predominant mind-set of our friends and neighbours
is one in which everything is transient and uncertain. But God has
revealed His plan for the universe and, as Ephesians 1:11 points out,

there is no risk that He will be thwarted. He is the One who works out everything in conformity with the purpose of His will.

Much of the failure of the Christian church to impact society in the last hundred years has stemmed from a loss of confidence in the authority of the Bible and the truth of its message. We are all affected by our culture, but Christian theologians have often been too ready to modify the truth of the Gospel to fit the prevailing philosophy. Early last century, modernism, which denied the existence of the supernatural, caused some theologians to try to "demythologize" the Scriptures – by removing the virgin birth, the resurrection and the Lord's miracles. When these are taken out, there is not much left!

> We are all affected by our culture, but Christian theologians have often been too ready to modify the truth of the Gospel to fit the prevailing philosophy.

In our own time, the *atheism* theme of 21st century society also denies these truths and the aggressively derisive way in which this is done can be unnerving to Christian believers. However, we have to realise that scientific theories and Christian faith are not necessarily incompatible: they are just answering different questions. Science is good at dealing with some of the "what" and the "how" questions. The "why" questions and the "end times" questions can be answered only on the basis of God's revelation of Himself in Christ in the Bible.

In addition, the *unrestricted life choices* theme that characterizes the post-modern worldview asserts that individuals should be free to decide what is "true" for themselves. This has influenced some Christians to develop beliefs about God and His ways that are taken from experiences and feelings, or from sources other than the Scriptures. Paul begins Ephesians and Colossians by setting out God's sure and certain purposes and our position in these purposes. Our experiences need to be interpreted by reference to that revelation, not the other way round.

But there is a second reason why it is important for us to understand doctrinal truth – it forms the basis for our lifestyle. In Colossians 1:3, Paul thanks the Lord for the believers at Colosse because he has heard of their faith and love, but in verse 5 he points out that these spring from the hope stored up for them in heaven. Contrary to common belief, Christians do not behave in a certain way in the selfish hope of getting to heaven; they have the sure and certain hope of eternal life and they live in *response* to the fact that they have been raised up to these incredible heights in Christ. They are attempting to be who they are in Christ, and live a life that is worthy of Him.

Unless we are rooted in an understanding of God's plans and our place in them, any instructions for living can appear arbitrary and we may be tempted to go along with moral changes as society evolves. The Christian church today is expanding, especially in developing countries, but there are concerns at the lack of depth in understanding the Scriptures. Without this, Christian belief and practice become fluid and can be distorted or corrupted by cultural and other influences.

> Unless we are rooted in an understanding of God's plans and our place in them, any instructions for living can appear arbitrary and we may be tempted to go along with moral changes as society evolves.

But "knowledge of God" involves more than understanding Christian theology. Since the Greek word used in Colossians 1:10 for "knowledge" has connotations of "acknowledgement," real knowledge of God is incomplete until it is lived out in our daily experience. Paul speaks of knowing God rather than knowing *about* God. His prayer for himself in Philippians 3:10 is that he may know Christ and the power of His resurrection. The power that raised Christ is available to us and in Ephesians and Colossians Paul prays that his readers may experience His "incomparably great power for us who believe" (Ephesians 1:19) and that they may be "strengthened with all power according to his glorious might" (Colossians 1:11). This is the power we will need to stand our ground in an ever-moving, fluid, post-modern society.

It is when we, as members of the body of Christ, try to follow the will of God by living in a way that is worthy of Him, that we experience the dynamic relationship with God that was promised by the Lord Jesus in John 17, and encounter the power of the Spirit in our everyday lives. The worthy walk also provides a positive contrast to the *image* and the *self-fulfilment* themes that are evident around us and which are so destructive to a wholesome society, as they put the 'self' first. So what does the worthy walk mean in terms of the way we live?

Bearing fruit in every good work:
Attitudes, behaviour and relationships

Attitudes

In trying to bear fruit in every good work, the first thing that Christians need is a right *attitude* because this governs all our conduct. In Ephesians 4 Paul reminds the believers that they were instructed to turn from the futile lifestyles of the pagans to follow the truth of Christ.

> You were taught, with regard to your former way of life, to put off your old self, which is being corrupted by its deceitful desires; to be made new in the *attitude* of your minds; and to put on the new self, created to be like God in true righteousness and holiness (Ephesians 4:22-24).

This radical renewal involves a shift in the *attitude* of our minds – from an earthly mind-set to a heavenly mind-set. The specific instructions that follow on in verses 25-32 flow directly from this new way of thinking:

> *Therefore* each of you must ... (Ephesians 4:25; see comment on verses 25-32 on pages 144-145)

And what is the essence of this attitude? We can see something of it in Philippians 2:

> ... being likeminded, having the same love, being one in spirit and purpose. Do nothing out of selfish ambition or vain conceit, but in humility consider others better than yourselves. Each of you should look not only to your own interests, but also to the

interests of others. Your *attitude* should be the same as that of Christ Jesus. (Philippians 2:2-5)

The Christian's attitude should be like that of the Lord, who placed the needs and interests of others before His own. He set aside His position of equality with God and went to the cross to benefit others. This approach should show itself within the Christian community in the way we encourage, help and are patient with everyone (1 Thessalonians 5:14). It will also lead to a spirit of joyfulness and thankfulness to God for His goodness and for each other.

But this outlook also shows itself in the way we interact with those outside the Christian community and this is where Christ's attitude is really counter-cultural. Most people spend a high proportion of their waking hours at work and it is there that Christians have the greatest opportunity to interact with non-Christians over a long period of time. It is therefore important that we develop the right attitude towards our colleagues, who may have no other connection with Christianity apart from us. So if we genuinely care for the needs of our colleagues and bosses, and prioritise their interests above our own, it will contrast with the attitudes we often find in others in the workplace. There the *self-fulfilment* theme of society is prominent. Advancement of self is all-important, frequently at the expense of colleagues. In addition, colleagues are often more concerned with the *image* that is projected – e.g. the image of a capable, diligent, company man or woman. The reality may be something else entirely! The Lord's way, which emphasises "speaking truthfully" (Ephesians 4:25), is so refreshingly different from the spin and distortion that we can encounter at work that it can be effective in attracting people to Him.

> It is important that we develop the right attitude towards our colleagues, who may have no other connection with Christianity apart from us.

But Christ's attitude also impacts on the nature of our casual conversations with friends and colleagues. Paul explains in Philippians 2:

Do everything without complaining or arguing, so that you may become blameless and pure, children of God without fault in a crooked and depraved generation, in which you shine like stars in the universe as you hold out the word of life (i.e. the gospel of salvation by grace through faith in Christ). (Philippians 2:14-16)

One of the features of our society is that, in spite of having so much, many people are always complaining and moaning. They grumble about their salary, whine about their boss, whinge about their working conditions, their neighbours and so it goes on. If Christians are not careful they can catch this insidious disease rather than practise "godliness with contentment, which is great gain" (1Timothy 6:6). If we show the attitude of Christ, we will be able to "shine like stars" and be more likely to be listened to when we "hold out the word of life."

It is important, then, for Christian believers, in trying to follow God's will, to adopt the right attitude because detailed patterns of behaviour will flow out from it. So what behaviour does the Lord want us to practise and what to avoid?

Behaviour that we should practise

Behaviour within the Christian community

As discussed in chapter 13, Ephesians 4-5 and Colossians 3 paint a picture of the way Christians should behave within their churches – with positive behaviour characteristics being contrasted with the negative alternatives. It is the Lord's will for Christian fellowships that they should be a loving and supportive environment, where kindness, forgiveness, honesty and mutual building-up are the order of the day rather than anger, malice, lying and slander. Tragically, down through the centuries, this has not been typical of some churches and a great deal of damage has been done as a result. The Lord Jesus, when He was on the earth, welcomed all who came to Him, even society's rejects like Zacchaeus and the woman at the well, and transformed their lives in the process. Similarly, Christian churches should be welcoming communities empowered by the Spirit to support people and help them to maturity in their faith.

Also crucial is the way we treat our leaders. When Paul wrote to Timothy and Titus, whom he had appointed as church leaders, he spelled out some of the qualities needed, including the need for temperance, self-control and gentleness. An aggressive and quarrelsome leader is a recipe for disaster, but what about church members? Grumbling at church leadership is common within Christian churches – whether it be at pastors, elders or deacons. Constant criticism is disheartening, destroys the harmony within the fellowship and undermines the Lord's work. Leaders should be supported and prayed for, so that they can be encouraged in their work.

The behaviour patterns that the Lord wants within our fellowships are very different from those that we see in the world around. The themes of *image, self-fulfilment and unrestricted life choices* that characterise our society should be absent from church life. The early church was planted in a hostile environment and one of the features that attracted people was the mutual care that existed within that community. This demonstrated what the Lord Jesus taught:

> By this all men will know that you are my disciples, if you love one another. (John 13:35)

Behaviour outside the Christian community

What sort of people should we be on a daily basis? It is the Lord's will that our lives should be conformed to the image of our Lord Jesus. There should be consistency in our behaviour seven days a week. The characteristics of truth, gentleness

> We are living in a society that is hostile to Christians and our message, and where some are keen to accuse Christians of wrongdoing. Thus our lives must be exemplary so that people will be more likely to listen to the Gospel.

and genuine practical care that we show to other Christians should be reflected in our dealings with our friends and colleagues outside the church. And this needs to be supported by our willingness to explain the Gospel to those we meet. The *atheism* theme means that we are living in a society that is hostile to Christians and our message, and where some are keen to accuse Christians of wrongdoing. Thus our lives must be exemplary so that people will be more likely to listen to the Gospel.

Peter wrote in the context of a similar society to ours. He states that our witnessing should be done in the right spirit – one that should characterize all our dealings with others.

> Always be prepared to give an answer to everyone who asks you to give the reason for the hope that you have. But do this with gentleness and respect, keeping a clear conscience, so that those who speak maliciously against your good behaviour in Christ may be ashamed of their slander. (1 Peter 3:15-16)

But it is not only as individuals that we can influence the world around us. Christians operating together, both as churches and as para-church groups, seeking to serve society in one way or another, have the potential to influence both local and national government. In this way they can bring about improvements in society.

Behaviour that we should avoid

Consumerism

1 John 2:15-17 contrasts the will of God with the world and its desires, which are summed up as:

> ... the cravings of sinful man, the lust of his eyes and the boasting of what he has and does...

The *image* and *self-fulfilment* themes of society really reveal themselves in our consumerism. In our consumer society, people validate themselves by spending, defining themselves by the kind of clothes they wear, the car they drive, and where they shop and eat. Self-worth is measured by material wealth and the extent to which they are admired or envied by others. It is easy for believers to be sucked into this way of thinking by the influence of our friends and the relentless advertising on TV and in other media. However, it is completely opposed to the way of Christ as it diverts our attention away from Him – from the things that are eternal, to the things which are transient.

We have been raised with Christ and our life is now hidden with Christ in God. Therefore we should set our hearts there, not on earthly things (Colossians 3:1-3). This materialistic outlook is having a harmful impact on our society. Oliver James, in his book *Affluenza*,[13] explores the corrosive effects that the obsessive pursuit of material possessions, and envious comparison of ourselves with others, are having on our mental health. Interestingly, Oliver James notes from his research that religious belief appears to be a strong vaccine against the 'affluenza virus.' The consumer society thrives on discontentment with our lot. However, if we have a proper understanding of God's purposes, and our place in them, we are less likely to lose sight of what has real value. We need the right attitude and His power in us to prevent this from happening, and to enable us to be content. Paul's attitude is a tremendous example to us and rings true down through the centuries:

> The consumer society thrives on discontentment. However, if we have a proper understanding of God's purposes we are less likely to lose sight of what has real value.

> I have learned the secret of being content in any and every situation, whether well fed or hungry, whether living in plenty or in want. I can do everything through him who gives me strength (Philippians 4:12-13).

Immorality

Peter's readers, though Jews, had lived as pagans before they became Christians and he reminds them of their past lifestyles, characterised by:

---

[13] *Affluenza*, Oliver James, Vermillion, 2007

... living in debauchery, lust, drunkenness, orgies, carousing and detestable idolatry. (1 Peter 4:3)

Paul also warns the Thessalonians against these practices:

> It is God's will that you should be sanctified: that you should avoid sexual immorality; that each of you should learn to control his own body in a way that is holy and honourable, not in passionate lust like the heathen, who do not know God. (1 Thessalonians 4:3-5)

As in Paul's time, *unrestricted life choices* lead to permissiveness and this is permeating our society. It means that young Christians today are under huge pressure to conform to the practices of their peers in relation to sexual behaviour, excessive drinking, and drug-taking. The damage caused in our society by a liberal approach to sex (in terms of unwanted pregnancies, disease and the destruction of relationships) is becoming increasingly apparent. The availability of internet pornography has meant that men, and in some cases women, are able to access material from their own homes and this is having a devastating effect on marriages and families.

Alcohol and drug abuse drive up crime figures and waste lives. How can we resist the pressures to conform? Firstly, by being aware of the Bible's unequivocal message that God's will for us is to avoid this behaviour. Secondly, by fostering communities of God's people where responsible Christian behaviour is practised. Members can be taught and encouraged to follow the Lord's revealed will, supported in resisting these pressures, and lovingly restored if they slip (Galatians 6:1). This leads us into the final aspect of bearing fruit – our relationships with other Christians and with unbelievers.

Relationships

In the Bible relationships are characterised by love (*agape*); an active, caring love. Chapter 13 explored in some detail the teaching of Paul on particular relationships. There are five people or groups we are told specifically to love:

- The Lord, who first loved us: expressed in thanksgiving, genuine worship and a commitment to obey Him (Matthew 22:37-38).
- Our families, particularly wives and husbands: husbands are to love their wives as Christ loved the church (Ephesians 5:25-33).
- Our fellow-Christian brothers and sisters: love for one another is a hallmark of our love for the Lord (1 John 4:20; John 13:35).
- Our neighbours and the world He created and sent the Lord Jesus to die for (Matthew 22:39; John 3:16).
- Our enemies: not repaying evil for evil, but blessing and praying for those who persecute us (Matthew 5:44; Romans 12:14,17).

Relationships within the Christian community

Love shows itself in a real commitment to one another in a number of ways. The church needs to be a welcoming community, where people can be cared for, feel accepted and not judged. There

> There should be a mutual accountability, where we encourage one another but at the same time are prepared to correct and instruct one another.

should be a mutual accountability, where we encourage one another but at the same time are prepared to correct and instruct one another. This can be extremely difficult: both to give and to take correction require a genuine openness and trust. The commitment to openness is at variance with the *image* theme that permeates our society and it also acts as a discipline against the danger of *unrestrained life choices* creeping into our lives.

Our commitment to other believers also needs to be expressed in tangible ways, including the offer of practical help, hospitality and financial resources. Perhaps most important of all is the willingness to give time to people – to pray with and for them, to listen to them, to empathise, to know them well enough to be able to engage at a deep and detailed level. It is not practical for us as limited human beings to have relationships of that depth with everyone in a fellowship. However, we all should have a few people with whom we relate at that level. Fellowship in a church should be characterised by such relationships so that no one falls through the cracks and is left on their own.

Relationships outside the Christian community

Although Christian fellowships should exist to worship the Lord and to offer support to members, we are not to be introspective groups. It is also the Lord's will that we should reach out into the locality where we live, to try to make a positive impact on the lives of the people who live there. The Lord's parable of the Good Samaritan in Luke 10 shows an application of the second great commandment: to love our neighbours as ourselves. In Matthew 5:16 He also tells the disciples that they are to let their light shine so that men will see their *good works* (rather than their piety) and glorify their Father in heaven.

Graham Cray in his book *Disciples & Citizens,* [14] identifies three dimensions of church life:

- *up* to God, to worship;
- *in* to one another to offer support and mutual accountability;
- *out* to the world to do good to our neighbours.

A fellowship that is balanced in this way can demonstrate a way of life that will have an enormously positive effect on the local community.

It is important to recognise that, in order to be effective in this way, *regular*, on-going commitment to people is required. Random acts of kindness are important but what is needed is the formation of long term committed relationships. There are many contemporary examples of churches being involved in projects benefiting their local communities – through the provision of child care, food banks, debt relief advice, legal and social services, etc.

Also, there are para-church organisations like Street Pastors, who operate in the major cities of the UK in partnership with the police,

---

[14] *Disciples and Citizens: A Vision for Distinctive Living,* Graham Cray, IVP, 2007, pp120-131

business and councils. Christians Against Poverty, a national debt-counselling charity works mainly through churches. Work of this nature provides the opportunity to speak of Christ, but the main aim is to bring the Christian community alongside people who need help.

Christian commitment to supportive relationships, both within and outside the community of believers, runs contrary to present day society's *self-fulfilment* theme because the primary aim in these

> Christian commitment to supportive relationships, both within and outside the community of believers, runs contrary to present day society's *self-fulfilment.*

caring relationships is the interests of the other person (Philippians 2:4). This commitment provides a powerful example of a better way of living. If we are going to influence people for Christ, Christians need to demonstrate that the way of the Lord Jesus provides a more fulfilling and attractive lifestyle than the secular alternatives (and it does – Acts 20:35!). Those outside the Christian fellowship are likely, initially at least, to be more influenced by how we live, as individuals and as a community, than by the truth or intellectual rigour of our message. The question is whether they will be attracted or repulsed by what they find. Sadly, it can be the latter.

However, work by individuals and churches tends to be at a neighbourhood level. To what extent is it God's will that we should attempt to influence society as a whole?

Christian impact on society as a whole

Should we engage?

What impact does the Lord expect us to have on our society? The Scriptures are clear that the kingdom of God will not appear on the earth until Christ returns. It is not our role to bring in that kingdom by totally transforming society. Biblical prophecy declares that the Lord will return with His heavenly army to deliver Israel from her enemies, and to establish His kingdom upon the earth. There is no indication that He will find a world waiting eagerly for His return. Indeed, specific passages such as Luke 18:8 suggest that there will be a dearth of true faith at that time.

Historically, Christians have been divided on the extent to which they should become involved with "the world". Organisations such as the Salvation Army and the various City Missions have, for many years, worked to help the needy in society. Individual Christians have also been at the forefront of many social improvements, such as the abolition of slavery and prison reform. On the other hand it has been argued that concentrating on social issues diverts us away from preaching the Gospel and bringing people to Christ, which is far more important. Besides, if the world is going to get worse and worse, and is one day going to be destroyed, then what is the point in trying to preserve it? Israel in the Old Testament was a theocracy, and many of the rules for that society are not relevant to us. The New Testament, it is argued, predominantly emphasises *personal* morality for individuals living within the Christian community and how they should relate to those they meet outside that community.

However, in the world of the 21st century such an attitude may no longer be appropriate. Although we are not expected to completely Christianise our society, the Lord Jesus does expect us to be salt and light *in* our society (Matthew 5:13-16). The context of salt (preserving from decay) and light (exposing wrong and showing the way to go) is "good deeds," for which men praise God. The Lord's command for us to love our neighbours means that we should want to improve our society. The first century church was a small, minority group in a totalitarian state and there was a limit to the impact they could be expected to have in society. Their "good deeds" would therefore be limited to work within the church and with their immediate personal contacts outside the fellowship.

> The context of salt (preserving from decay) and light (exposing wrong and showing the way to go) is "good deeds," for which men praise God.

Our situation is different for two main reasons. Firstly, the growth of global communications and the ease with which we can access information, mean that our awareness of needs, injustices and problems has widened far beyond our local area. We cannot claim we do not know what is going on.

Secondly, we live in democracies, and if we make the time and effort, we can make our views known to government and other public bodies, which may bring about broader change.

In the first section of the book we noted that the Lord's will for Israel included a concern for justice and fairness in their society. We also noted His anger at the oppression of vulnerable people such as the widow, the fatherless and the alien. If we are aware of similar evils in our society (and we are) and we are able to do something about them (and many are), then we will not be following the Lord's will if we turn a blind eye to them.

Potential areas for Christian engagement

The scope for Christians to bring a positive influence is vast. The areas that are briefly discussed here are the tip of the iceberg. But it is important to realise that, although the needs are enormous, the opportunities for us to become involved have never been greater. There are needs at local levels but many of the problems are national, or even global, in nature and can be addressed only through government activity. We therefore need to be prepared to engage with governments, the media, and others in authority to make our views known and influence policies. The following are examples of areas for potential Christian involvement.

Protection of the environment

In the Garden of Eden, Adam was told to nurture and care for a creation that God pronounced as "good." Since then, man has abused his God-given mandate and exploited the world and its resources. In the future, the Lord Jesus will return to establish His kingdom upon the earth. Some of the Old Testament prophets (e.g. Isaiah, in chapters 11 and 60) describe the glorious situation in that kingdom, predicting that the earth will be full of the knowledge of the Lord. If this is the earth's destiny then we have a responsibility to look after and not to pollute it or waste finite resources.

Since the Lord created all living creatures, and everything was created for Christ's glory, how can we be uncaring about the extinction of species as a result of our greed-motivated destruction of habitats? Christian people should be at the forefront of conservation, but they can bring an added dimension – unlike some members of the New Age movement, Christians can distinguish between the creation and the Creator, and not see the earth as something to be worshipped.

Fair trade

The fair trade movement, heavily influenced by Christian organisations such as Tear Fund, was one of the success stories of the 20th century. The introduction of free trade markets in the developing world, can, in fact, damage these countries. The dumping of cheap products into developing countries and their markets can destroy indigenous industries and price local producers out of the market. It has been recognised that *fair* trade, rather than *free* trade, is what is necessary to ensure that local producers are given a fair price for their goods. This enables businesses to flourish and restores dignity and self-sufficiency to communities.

However, although most of our supermarkets carry an extensive stock of fairly traded goods, there is still much to be done in this area to broaden the scope of product range. Increased globalisation has encouraged multi-nationals to set up bases in developing countries, and it has been argued that these can cause major damage to the local industries. For example, in the Niger delta there are allegations that fish ponds, drinking water and farms have been contaminated by the activities of Shell Nigeria.[15] A number of activist groups are involved in trying to stop such practices: Christians need to be lending their voices too.

---

[15] "Shell: Clean-up goes on for Niger Delta – and oil company's reputation," *The Guardian*, 4 February 2011, p32

Justice in society

In the Old Testament we saw it was God's will for Israel to be concerned for the vulnerable in society, with a recurring emphasis on the widows, orphans and aliens. In our time there are similar vulnerable groups – the long term unemployed, single mothers, addicts and asylum seekers. Local needs can be tackled by local fellowships, but we must lift our eyes to identify the root causes of these problems. In the UK and the US in particular, the earnings gap between the highest paid and the lowest paid has widened enormously. Many still have a misplaced trust in free markets to regulate society, but market forces tend to make the rich richer and the poor poorer.

In the Old Testament God's provision of the Jubilee regulations was intended to prevent poverty from becoming institutionalised in Israel. In our society "selfish capitalism" has created an underclass who have never worked and have no prospect of doing so. Instead, successive generations are locked into a cycle of lack of opportunity, addiction and hopelessness. As we write, both the UK government and the opposition are calling for "responsible" or "moral" capitalism to curb the worst excesses. There are no quick fixes for the problems of anti-social behaviour by business, but Christians need to contribute a Biblical perspective to the debate, focusing their arguments on the welfare of the underprivileged.

> There are no quick fixes for the problems of anti-social behaviour by business, but Christians need to contribute a Biblical perspective to the debate, focusing their arguments on the welfare of the underprivileged.

Debt problems

Social pressures created by consumerism have encouraged individuals (and governments) to borrow beyond their means. This has been encouraged by global financial institutions keen to grow profitability by lending, often to those who have little prospect of repaying the loan. The problems resulting from this policy are now creating homelessness, family breakdown, and despair.

As with the issue of justice, individuals can be helped by groups (such as Christians Against Poverty) who are prepared to provide financial advice, support, and to negotiate with creditors on their behalf. However, something more needs to be done. Christian virtues such as contentment and thrift need to be re-introduced to mainstream thinking. The Jubilee Debt Campaign, which arose from the Jubilee 2000 project, in which Christians were heavily involved, is seeking the complete cancellation of unpayable debt owed to rich countries by poor. There have been calls for this also to be introduced at a personal level in the UK.

Moral issues

In the last forty years the UK has increasingly been characterised by moral confusion, largely as a consequence of the growing effect of relativism in people's thinking, resulting in the absence of moral authority. Public life also has been plagued by scandals and alleged misconduct on a breath-taking scale - the near collapse of the banking system caused largely by uncontrolled risk-taking, the scandal of parliamentary expenses, the phone-hacking and alleged breaches of ethical standards by members of the press, and the looting and destruction following the riots in the summer of 2011. The *image, self-fulfilment* and *unrestrained life choices* in contemporary thinking are not producing a supportive society. In our culture the outlook is becoming increasingly similar to the times of the Judges when "everyone did that which was right in his own eyes" (Judges 17:6, *KJV*).

The forces of *aggressive atheism* are trying to undermine Christian influence on society, apparently in the interests of "freedom." The abandonment of Christian principles has created a vacuum into which has flooded *unrestrained life choices*. This has resulted in the spread of promiscuity, excessive drinking, drug-taking, and pornography. However there are also the more subtle attitudes like greed, materialism and self-aggrandisement that are an undercurrent to 21st century life. In addition, there are proposals to relax regulations so as to allow same sex marriages, to increase the availability of abortion and to permit assisted suicide. How many of these would be in harmony with the will of God?

As suggested earlier, minority groups in a society tend to protect themselves in one of two ways. Firstly, they can become like chameleons and blend into the society by adopting its ways and becoming indistinguishable from everyone else.[16] As we consider the will of God for His people, as revealed in Scripture, it is clear that this approach is untenable. The Lord expects us to be different – not to be conformed to the world but to be transformed by the renewing of our minds (Romans 12:2).

The second approach for minority groups is to take on a 'bunker' mentality and retreat from the world, keeping themselves separate from it and socialising only with group members, developing their own culture and norms. Although some Christians have taken this approach, it is doubtful that it can be reconciled with the Lord's command to be salt and light in the world. He expects us to become involved and have a positive influence where we can.

There is a huge need for the caring Christian voice to be heard in the world and in our democratic society we have an opportunity to make an impact, if we are wise in our approach. So how should we engage with society at large? This will be addressed in the next section.

How should we engage?

Many of the practices we find in society today go against the Scriptures, especially on moral issues. Although we can declare God's judgment on sin, we cannot expect to persuade the secular authorities and the non-believers, who make up the vast majority of our society, by simply quoting the Bible at them. If we do this, we shall find that it carries no weight as they do not recognise Biblical authority. If we are to encourage changes for the better we shall need to base our arguments on other grounds.

---

[16] See *Chameleon or Tribe? Recovering authentic Christian Community*, Richard Keyes, IVP, 1999.

Fortunately the bases for living set out in Scripture are not arbitrary, but are designed by our Creator to form the basis of a benevolent and stable society. Therefore it is possible to defend them using health, sociological or psychological arguments. For example, we can argue for a monogamous marriage relationship between a man and a woman as being the bedrock of a stable society and the most supportive environment for bringing up children, based on the considerable research that has been done in this area.

The integration of message and action

So if we are not able to use Scripture as the primary basis for our arguments, what is the relationship between our social action and the Christian message? This is one of the most difficult issues facing Christians wanting to engage in these issues. There may be a temptation to use social action as a means of preaching the Gospel. In this case, the practical help and support offered would really be the bait to bring people in to the sound of the Gospel. If that were so, the preaching of that message would be the hidden agenda of the Christians. Such an approach is likely to lead to resentment and suspicion of Christians generally, and to be counter-productive in the long run.

At the other extreme there is a danger that the social action becomes totally divorced from the Christian message of the church. This can happen, particularly when Christian workers link themselves with secular charities or groups who are trying to achieve similar social ends. On the one hand, this is understandable as there is no logic in "re-inventing the wheel" by setting up a new group to duplicate the work of an existing organisation. However, such an arrangement can lead to clashes of values between the Christians and the non-Christians. There is also a risk that the distinctive Christian perspective may be lost and we become just part of another voluntary group.

So how can we ensure that the care and action are authentic without losing sight of the Gospel message? Firstly, it is preferable to form a specific Christian group for a particular purpose or attach ourselves to an existing Christian group. Organisations like Christians

Against Poverty work almost like a quasi-franchise operation, which can be introduced in different places. Secondly, we must always remember that it is the power of Christ that changes lives. We want to introduce people to Him, not to expand our church, but to improve their lives here and now and to bring them eternal life.

So although practical help is offered without strings attached, the practical help must be re-enforced by the message that the Lord Jesus can liberate from bondage and bring love and meaningful living to anyone.

> We must always remember that it is the power of Christ that changes lives.

For example, someone addicted to alcohol or pornography may not respond if we quote Romans 13:13, to show the Lord's condemnation of such behaviour. We may need to encourage them to follow a recovery programme by pointing out the health and social problems caused by their addiction. However, they do need to hear that the Lord Jesus is the great deliverer from all addiction and that they should trust in Him.

Models for Christian influence

Christians can bring their influence to bear on society either individually or as part of a group.

Engaging as individuals in a local context

We have already considered how Christians can be a positive influence in their neighbourhood and place of work by their attitudes, the way they behave, and the relationships they form with their neighbours and colleagues.

Christians may also frequently find themselves in places where there are practices which they would regard as ethically dubious, at best, or morally wrong, at worst. Here again they may be able to be a force for good. A Christian doctor, faced with a young pregnant patient who is in a panic and wanting an abortion, may be able to give the patient time to talk through the issues and see that there are alternatives available. Christians working in business may also be in a position to encourage an ethical approach in dealing with staff, suppliers and customers.[17]

However, there are a number of problems in this area for Christians. A permissive society is in danger of becoming a prescriptive society. For example, a number of countries now permit same sex marriages. Christians who work as Registrars, who are called to perform such marriages may feel they are unable to do so and some may lose their jobs as a result of this. In the UK at present the issue of same sex marriages is being debated and the Government, recognising the dilemma for faith groups, is trying to ensure that religious groups or individual ministers are not forced to conduct such marriages against their conscience. However, there are concerns that equal opportunities legislation will undermine such a stance.

What are Christians to do if they find themselves in this situation? Firstly, they must conduct themselves in the correct manner, not just telling it as it is, but "speaking the truth in love" (Ephesians 4:15).

> Let your conversation be always full of grace, seasoned with salt, so that you may know how to answer everyone. (Colossians 4:6)

The consequences of taking such a stand, even if we present our case lovingly and graciously, can be serious and there are no easy answers. Peter and John, ordered by the Jewish authorities not to speak or teach in the name of Jesus responded by saying:

> "We must obey God rather than men!" (Acts 5:29)

The apostles had the choice of conforming to what the authorities wanted or confronting them. They chose to obey God rather than men, but the inevitable consequence of confrontation was punishment and on this occasion they were flogged (Acts 5:40). Yet we read:

---

[17] See *Going by the Book: the Bible and Christian Ethics*, Neil Messer; Canterbury Press.

The apostles left the Sanhedrin, rejoicing because they had been counted worthy of suffering disgrace for the Name. (Acts 5:41)

And Peter also has much to say about such suffering for good.

But how is it to your credit if you receive a beating for doing wrong and endure it? But if you suffer for doing good and you endure it, this is commendable before God. (1 Peter 2:20)

It is better, if it is God's will, to suffer for doing good than for doing evil. (1 Peter 3:17)

However, if you suffer as a Christian, do not be ashamed, but praise God that you bear that name. (1 Peter 4:16)

Paul wrote that "everyone who wants to live a godly life in Christ Jesus will be persecuted" (2 Timothy 3:12), and we might well change that last word to 'prosecuted' in a prescriptive society. This is a sobering thought for Christians in the 21st century. We who live in a democratic country, however decadent it may be, may well be forced to confront the authorities and refuse to obey some of the laws which we believe are contrary to the Lord's will. In such circumstances we must conduct ourselves with love and grace, but we will have to accept the consequences.

Engaging as individuals in a wider context

In recent years there has been a huge increase in the opportunity for individuals to express their views on current issues. First, the development of communications technology provides a wide range of media through which views can be expressed – e-mails, blogging, chat rooms and so on, and some Christians engage regularly with politicians, civic authorities, newspapers or television companies, to provide a Christian perspective on issues of the day.

In addition, members of the public are now encouraged by lobby groups to express their views individually. Political organisations themselves are keen to understand the views of their constituents. The more we become involved in these activities, the more impact our views have but, generally, in the 20th century, the Christian voice was rather muted. May it become more vocal in the 21st!

However, if we are going to use these media for expressing our views we should not only complain about things that concern us; we should also give compliments and encouragement where there have been programmes or articles that are positive and helpful. Too often Christians are perceived as always being negative. Our engagement with politicians and the media should be balanced.

For example, Easter 2008 saw the BBC's excellent production of *The Passion*, which was screened on British television, and in December 2010 the BBC produced a first class, four part drama *The Nativity*. If we want more Christian programmes on TV then we must let the companies know that we watch them, and let them know of our approval. If we remain silent, we shall achieve nothing. The opportunities for us to engage are much greater than they were twenty years ago and, if more Christians take the time to express their views, they will have an impact.

> The opportunities for us to engage are much greater than they were twenty years ago and, if more Christians take the time to express their views, they will have an impact.

Engaging as part of a group

In recent years there has been a massive growth in the number of Christian charities and social enterprise companies which are focused on social issues and concerns over poverty and justice. The programmes at Christian festivals, such as Greenbelt and Spring Harvest, include sessions devoted to these issues. There has been a proliferation of books on the subject, providing Scriptural backing for social engagement and showing how it can be done. Christian organisations contribute articles and advertisements in magazines explaining the work they are doing and requesting prayer and other support.

A huge number of churches regard social action in their local community, and engagement at a national and international level, as a major part of their programmes, running everything from local debt counselling ministries to 'fair trade fortnights' selling consumable items and publicising the work of Fair Trade. Umbrella organisations like Evangelical Alliance engage with politicians at a national level and encourage networking of their members with one another to improve the effectiveness of their work.

> It is not our task to bring in Christ's kingdom upon the earth. The kingdom of the world will become the kingdom of our Lord and of His Christ when He returns (Revelation 11:15). But we can achieve *something*.

There is, therefore, a wide range of opportunities for Christians to have a positive influence on our society to work to reduce the levels of injustice and oppression, and to fight moral evil where we see it. From the Old Testament we can catch the vision of God's blueprint for a society that is honouring to Him. In the New Testament also, the Lord Jesus' re-iteration of the command to love our neighbour as ourselves needs to be interpreted in a wide context. The parable of the Good Samaritan, told by Jesus to illustrate the point He was making, shows that our "neighbour" is basically anyone we come across who needs help. In our era of global communication we have no excuse for claiming that we are not aware of needs.

The problem is that the task is so overwhelming. How can we hope to really make a difference? Besides, there are other voices who are trying to influence society in ways that are not in line with the Lord's will for humanity. What can we, as a relatively small group, hope to do? We have already suggested that it is not our task to bring in Christ's kingdom upon the earth, and completely Christianise society. The kingdom of the world will become the kingdom of our Lord and of His Christ when He returns (Revelation 11:15). But we can achieve *something*. There is one important principle to follow:

What progress can we expect to make? We may have a Biblical ideal that we would like to see operating in our country. This may be the 'best' option and we might choose to adopt this for ourselves, as Christians. However, in a secular society, although we may find it impossible to achieve this universally, there may be something 'better' that could be achieved.

Two examples illustrate how this approach might operate. Firstly, Christians in various countries have been working on reducing the time limits for abortions. At present in the UK the limit is up to the 24th week of gestation and recently a move to reduce this to 22 weeks was rejected by the British Medical Association. Ideally, Christians might prefer abortions to be performed only in the event of particular medical problems (or even not at all) but reducing the time limit may be regarded as 'better' than the present position. The 'best' may be no abortions. But in a secular society that may be impossible. Thus Christians supporting a decrease to 22 weeks are not saying they agree with abortion; they simply want something 'better.'

Another issue is the 9.00 pm watershed that exists on British Television. After this time swearing, explicit sex and violence can be shown, the theory being that by that time children are in bed. We may prefer that these things were not shown at all (the 'best') but realistically this is not going to happen. Perhaps we should instead campaign for the watershed to be made later – say 10.00 pm (the 'better'). This is a very difficult issue because, arguably, the watershed is largely irrelevant since programmes can be downloaded to computers and mobile phones and watched at any time of day. This is one of the downsides of the convenience of programme availability. Perhaps we should be making a case for the limitation of that availability to protect those who are vulnerable.

In summary...

The Lord has revealed the mystery of His will for the cosmos in the Scriptures – to head up everything in the Lord Jesus Christ. He has also adopted us as His children through the work of the Lord Jesus and qualified us to share in the inheritance of the saints. Having given us a glimpse of our identity and our destiny, He has revealed His will for the kind of people we should be, so that we can live in a way that is worthy of who we are in the Lord Jesus.

He calls us to an understanding of the truths in relation to Himself and to an acknowledgement of His will in our lives. He wants us to work out our salvation in the community of believers in terms of our attitudes to others, the behaviour patterns we practise in the fellowship, and the relationships we develop with one another, and with Him. These enable the members of the community to grow in the knowledge of Christ and to become like Him until we reach the level of spiritual maturity that He wants of us. A Christian community which follows His will in these ways will shine like a beacon and show the world outside how life can potentially be lived, and will attract people to the Lord. This is all the more vital in the 21st century, where the ungodly attitudes of *obsession with image, self-fulfilment,* and *unrestrained life choices* are blighting character and decaying our society.

But His will for us is not that we should live in a bunker and be a 'holy huddle', aloof from the world and caring only for other Christians. He calls us to be salt in a decaying world. As members of Christ's body on the earth we hold out the word of life, ministering His truth and grace in a society in which the forces of *atheism* are increasingly hostile to His message. To do this effectively we must avoid both the ungodly attitudes of consumerism, with its related evils, and the immorality that fills our newspapers and TV screens and which is accepted as "normal" behaviour in Western countries. It may be unsettling for us as Christians to realise that many young Muslims in the UK today are openly declaring that they have rejected the values of our society.

Sadly, some of them have turned to violence and hatred of our country as a result. The Lord asks us also to reject the evil in our culture, but His will is that we love those who are lost rather than curse or judge them. We need to have the same attitude as the Lord Jesus Christ in loving our neighbours, whoever they are. This needs to be done consistently by committing ourselves to long term engagement with the communities in which we find ourselves, so as to offer help and support where it is needed.

But we need to widen our scope beyond the immediate locality. There are national and global issues of poverty, injustice and oppression, and the Lord has given us, in the Scriptures, a picture of the kind of society that is pleasing to Him. Living in a democracy, in a world of global communication, we cannot claim ignorance and powerlessness as excuses for not speaking out for the truth and taking action to relieve the vulnerable and the victims in our world.

Seeking the will of God is a major priority for Christians. In the Scriptures He has set out His will for us – the kind of people He wants us to be and how He wants us to behave. He has adopted us as His sons and daughters in the Lord Jesus Christ, and He calls us to live in a way that is appropriate to our identity as members of His family. This means setting our minds on the heavenly places where Christ is seated and where we truly belong; it means not following the mindset and practices of the world because:

> The world and its desires pass away, but the man who does the will of God lives forever. (1 John 2:17)

Appendix
A will for everything?

Does God have a detailed plan for our lives?

Some Christians believe that God has a very specific will for every aspect of our lives, like a detailed plan mapped out from the day we were born. This means that God has decided in advance who He wants us to marry (if anyone), where we should study and work, where we should live, which car we should drive, and so on. Therefore, in approaching these decisions we pray for the Lord to reveal His will to us. In one sense this is good because we need to consider the Lord's perspective in all aspects of our lives. But if there is a 'right' person to marry or a 'right' place to work, we can become fearful of making a wrong decision which might lead us out of God's will. However, there is, in fact, little in Scripture to support the view that our lives are mapped out in advance.

One of the difficulties from our standpoint is that we are bounded by time, whereas God is not. His foreknowledge means that He knows what will happen, what we will decide and what we will do, so He can work in our circumstances to His glory, provided we are trying to live in His ways. However, His foreknowledge of what is going to happen does not mean that it is His will for it to happen. The Lord Jesus knew beforehand that Peter would deny Him three times; this does not mean that it was His will that Peter should do so.

So what passages in Scripture are used to support the view that God has specific plans for each of us? One of the commonly used verses is Jeremiah 29:11

> This is what the Lord says: "When seventy years are completed for Babylon, I will come to you and fulfil my gracious promise to bring you back to this place. For I know the plans I have for you," declares the Lord, "plans to prosper you and not to harm you, plans to give you hope and a future." (Jeremiah 29:10-11)

However, it is important to see that the context of these verses shows that God is not speaking of *individuals*. He is speaking of the restoration of the *nation* of Israel following their seventy year exile in Babylon. There is no doubt that He had a plan for the nation: they were to be a kingdom of priests, but there is no suggestion that there was a detailed purpose for every individual in that nation.

It is sometimes argued that the experiences of biblical characters such as Abraham, Moses, and Paul show that God does have a detailed blueprint for our lives. But very few of us are an Abraham or a Paul, and the detailed instructions given to these pioneers related to the major roles they had to play in the outworking of God's unfolding purposes, not to every facet of their lives. It is interesting to note that Paul nowhere in his writings suggests that Christians should seek the Lord's predetermined will for every aspect of their lives.

So does God not care what we do – whom we marry or where we work? Indeed He does, but as we have tried to suggest in this book, He expresses His will to us in Scripture by telling us *how* we should live and the kind of people we should be. The Scriptures set out principles and the Lord asks us to work through them with the guidance of the Holy Spirit, whom He has given us. In this way we can develop the spiritual wisdom needed to apply the principles of His will to our situations. This is part of what Paul means when he tells us to:

> ...work out your salvation with fear and trembling, for it is God who works in you to will and to act according to his good purpose. (Philippians 2:12,13)

With respect to choosing a marriage partner, Paul has advice for widows:

> A woman is bound to her husband as long as he lives. But if her husband dies, *she is free to marry anyone she wishes*, but he must belong to the Lord. (1 Corinthians 7:39)

Apart from the caveat that her new husband must be a believer, the woman can marry "anyone she wishes." There is no suggestion that there is one specific person 'chosen' for her by God.

So, as we contemplate marriage, the primary question is whether our prospective partner is a believer. If not, it is not the Lord's will that we should marry them. If they are a believer, we may marry them but spiritual wisdom (and common sense!) might suggest to us that their priorities or personalities are not compatible with ours and this could lead to problems in the marriage. We may be unwise to go ahead and, if we do so, we may have difficulties, but we shall not have done wrong.

Similarly, in issues of studying and career there may be particular industries that it would not be the Lord's will for us to work in, such as tobacco or gambling or the sex trade. However, our decision not to work in these areas comes from the general teaching of Scripture.

When we come to specific jobs, place of work or promotion, we need to ask ourselves questions such as: 'Will this position help me to serve the Lord better or will it have a negative impact on my witness and service?' For example, if we are thinking of working for a company that is known to follow sharp practices we may decide to go there to try to change the culture. Alternatively, we may feel that there would be too much pressure on us to do what is unethical and therefore we should not take the job. That decision is determined, again, by a knowledge of God's revelation of His will in Scripture, by spiritual discernment in knowing our strengths and weaknesses, and by realistically assessing the situation.

Does God care which car we drive? He may not have any preferences between a Volkswagen and a Volvo, but we do know that He detests pride and wants us to practise prudent financial stewardship. Therefore if we are driving an ostentatious car that we cannot really afford, as a status symbol, then He is unlikely to be pleased with us. Once more, our decisions are made by applying the principles of His revealed will to the situation.

In making decisions we need prayerfully to weigh up all the pros and cons, all the advantages and disadvantages, and, with the God-given wisdom that we have, make a choice. No doubt in the process of time we may discover that some of the decisions we have made have not been for the best, and some may even have been serious misjudgements. However, as time goes by, and as we develop in our understanding of the Lord and His ways, we should make better personal decisions. This is part of the maturing process and a test to see where our priorities lie. However, whatever our decision may be over such issues, we should be much more concerned about putting the will of God into practice, and living a life that pleases Him, than we are about our personal circumstances. Undoubtedly, the Lord is interested in the key issues of our lives, such as where we live or which job we do, but we can serve Him and put His will into practice no matter wherever we live and whatever we do for a living.

Are there ever specific things God wants us to do?

So if God does not have a detailed, predetermined plan covering all details of our lives, are there ever specific things He wants us to do? The answer must be 'yes'. In Ephesians 2:10 Paul states that we are:

> ... created in Christ Jesus to do good works, which God prepared in advance for us to do.

These will certainly include all the good works listed later in Ephesians and in the rest of Scripture. Each of us has different talents and we operate in different spheres of influence, so we may find ourselves faced with situations that are specific to us and not covered in Scripture. We may find ourselves in circumstances when we *alone* can do some 'good thing' for someone. In that case, there is little doubt that the Lord would expect us to do it, without further guidance.

Sometimes, of course, it is not quite so clear. Perhaps we are not aware of a need, but in situations like this we may feel prompted to visit someone or phone them and, when we do, we find they are in need of help. As we look back on our lives many of us can think of times when, seemingly by chance, we have been in the right place to help another. These may be part of the "good works, which God prepared in advance for us to do", and it may well have been His Spirit prompting us.

On occasion, then, the Lord has to put it into our hearts to do something for Him, either because we are not aware of the need or because we are too distracted by our own concerns to notice the need or recognize our ability to meet it. However, we should not seek these prompts as there is no guarantee that we will receive them. There is a danger of taking a Scriptural example of where God has interacted directly with an individual and expecting Him to deal in the same way with us.

For example, Gideon, in Judges 6:36-40, tested God's presence with him by putting out a fleece to see whether it attracted dew or not. Nowadays we may not put out a fleece, but we might look for 'signs' to help us to find God's will – e.g. 'If a letter from X arrives today I will know that God wants me to...' In fact we have no authority to do this and will run into difficulties if we try.

Similarly, we may think we can get guidance as Paul did on his second missionary journey. There, somehow or other, the Spirit prevented Paul from going either to Asia or Bithynia (Acts 16:6-8). Later he was given a vision to go on to Macedonia, which he did (Acts 16:9-10). Subsequently he was given another vision, encouraging him to preach and stay in Corinth (Acts 18:9-11).

However, we have no instruction to look for visions and, indeed, there seems to have been no such guidance on Paul's first missionary journey. Having been sent on their way by the Holy Spirit (Acts 13:4), they went off to Cyprus. This was a sane and sensible first step. Barnabas had family there, and there were already Christians there who had been to Antioch (Acts 4:36; 11:19-20).

When they completed their tour of the island they decided to cross the sea and go up into Galatia, to such places as Pisidian Antioch, Iconium, Lystra and Derbe. Again we are told of no guidance being given. From the human point of view, this was another good decision. The Jews of that region were Hellenised. Some failed to circumcise their children (Acts 16:3) and not one of these cities, or this region, is listed in Acts 2:9-11, indicating that the Jews there may well have been indifferent towards their faith. This would be a challenge, but the Jews there needed to know about Jesus and, if none was going up to the feasts of Jerusalem, where they would hear about Him from Peter and the other apostles working there, then Paul would take them the message. This was how Paul decided he would carry out the commission given him on the road to Damascus: "This man is my chosen instrument to carry my name before the Gentiles and their kings and before the people of Israel" (Acts 9:15).

Thus, what the Lord wants from us is to make sensible and sometimes courageous and selfless decisions, based on prayer and spiritual wisdom. Sometimes He may prompt us to specific actions by placing an idea in our minds but, even though God did give guidance through visions, dreams and other direct communication to some of the leaders, for much of the time they were left to their own devices, to work things out for themselves by following the principles laid down.

Are there dangers in seeking God's specific will for everything?

Is there any harm in trying to seek out God's will for every aspect of our lives? It is, after all, important that we do consider Him when making major life-decisions, but there are dangers in thinking God has a specific will for every minor aspect of our lives and that we have to strive to find His will.

First, apart from the sheer impracticability of praying for guidance for the many decisions we make each day, asking for specific answers to everything shows a lack of trust in the clear guidance He has given us in Scripture. We cease to think through the principles the Lord has revealed to us and use Him like a satellite guidance system in a car, telling us which direction we should go and which turning to take. In effect, what we are doing, is seeking out the secret things relating to what is going to happen in the future. These are hidden in God, and Moses reminded the Israelites:

The secret things belong to the Lord our God, but the things revealed belong to us and to our children forever, that we may follow all the words of this law. (Deuteronomy 29:29)

The Israelites' priority was to follow the revealed will of God through the Law, as we discussed in the first section of the book. To go beyond this is Adam's sin of wanting to be like God and to know the secret things which are hidden. Today millions of people read horoscopes, practise astrology or consult mediums before making decisions. These are all pagan practices attempting to access the secret things in order to obtain reassurance on the rightness of any course of action. Christians who, in some way or other, seek God's will as a basis for every decision, no matter how trivial, are in danger of giving up their God-given wisdom and abrogating their responsibility to think through the application of the principles and teaching set out in Scripture.

Secondly, looking for guidance in all situations will hinder us from thinking through God's revelation of Himself and applying the revelation of His will contained in Scripture. That will slow our spiritual growth. God's aim is for us to be "conformed to the likeness of His Son" (Romans 8:29) and to be "mature, attaining to the full measure of the fulness of Christ" (Ephesians 4:13). The Lord, by His Spirit, is trying to develop godly thinking in us, to direct our minds so that we will understand His revealed will, apply it and acknowledge it on a daily basis.

If we live relying on *ad hoc* prompts from the Lord on what to do in any situation, there is a risk that we become susceptible to impulses that we wrongly attribute to the Lord and which may not be consistent with the Scriptures. We may feel that God is calling us to do certain things when, in fact, the Bible has already revealed His displeasure at them. This can lead to inconsistency, which does not honour Him. There is no merit in eagerly asking the Lord to reveal to us whom we should marry if we are having sexual relationships before marriage; there is no benefit in asking the Lord to guide us to the job He wants us to do if we are lazy in our work or unhelpful to our colleagues.

Thirdly, constantly waiting for guidance can lead to indecision in our lives. If we ask God to reveal His will to us for everything we do and no obvious answers are forthcoming, we may be afraid to take a decision. This can result in inertia and a great deal of unnecessary stress because we fear we need to be careful that we do not make the wrong decision and so be 'out of His will' for us. This leads to the last point.

If we believe that *everything* is planned in advance for us, what happens when we fail or make the wrong decision? Are we no longer in His purposes? Is there a 'Plan B'? If so, could it be that Plan B was the real plan all along? We can tie ourselves completely in knots over issues like that. Sadly, some Christians who have failed (and all of us have to some extent) feel that they are living in God's 'second best' for their lives. This is not a helpful outlook. In fact, it is not just the big decisions that we can handle unwisely. It is a sad reality that none of us follows the Lord perfectly on a daily basis. We are constantly doing things that do not please Him and failing to take opportunities that He gives us. However, His 'grandstand' view of our lives means that He can take account of the twists and turns in our pilgrimage and work in *all* things "for the good of those who love him, who have been called according to his purpose" (Romans 8:28). The context of this verse is our destiny to become like Christ. Wherever we are, no matter what we have done and what decisions we have made, the Lord in His grace will work in our situation for our good and for His glory.

The Lord has given us clear teaching in the Bible as to what His will is. He has also given each one of us talents. He wants to see how well we will obey His commands and how well we will use those talents for His glory. Whatever we decide to do, specifically, is largely up to us. However, our desire should be to please Him and serve Him so that at the end, when He assesses our stewardship, He will say:

"Well done, good and faithful servant!" (Matthew 25:23)

Index of Scripture References

Genesis
1:28-29 15
2:15,20 14
6:5,7,11 14
9:2-4 15
9:5-6 16
12 25
12:1-3 18
13:14-17 18
15:1-7 18
15:2-3 19
15:6 19,81,
 104,105
15:9 18
15:13-14 22
16:1-2 19
17:1-22 18
17:10 18
17:24 105
18:1-5 18
19:29 19
20:5-6 17
21:13 19
22:1-14 19
22:15-18 18
25:11 19
26:5,12 19
28:10-22 19
31:30-34 20
31:42 20
35:1-2 20
35:11-12 20
39:3,21,23 20
45:7 21
48:21 21
50:24-25 21

Exodus
2:24-25 22
3:6-10 22,23

12:14 23
12:48-49 23
16:13 33
16:29-30 23
16:31 33
17:6 33
18 36
18:13-26 26
18:15-16 23
18:15 42
18:15-22 70
18:19-22 23
19 26
19:4-6 24
22:28 92,117
20:3 71
22:28 30
23:1-9 52
23:6-9 27
23:10-11 28
23:13 28
28:30 34
34:6-7 82

Leviticus
6 115
6:18 92
6:24-26 82
12:5-8 70
19:15 55
19:35-36 55
22:31-33 28
23:27 80
24:10-16 30
25:8-28 28
26:3-4 28

Numbers
1:1 26
9:1 26

9:8-14 30
11:25 36
11:31 33
12:5-8 36
15:32-36 30
15:39-41 29
20:11 33
27:18-21 35
36:13 26

Deuteronomy
1:1 26
4:1-2 29
4:6-8 29,70,
 71
5:16 152
6:13,16 77
8:3 76
8:4 33
8:6-8 34
10:16 72
13:1-3 36
15:11 55
17:8-11 30,31
17:9-10 34
17:18-20 33
18:17-18 37
18:20-22 36
23:24-25 80
28 33,38
28:1-14 31
28:15-18 32
28:25 32
28:36-37 32
28:43-44 32
28:45 45
28:45-46 32,
 33
28:49-50
 32,45

28:64 45
29:29 204
30:15-16 32
33:8 35

Joshua
1:7-8 39
5 39
7 35
8 41
8:31 39
23:6-7 40
23:16 40

Judges
2:7 40
2:10-11 40
6:36-40 203
10:6-7 40
10:10-11:33
 40
17:6 189

1 Samuel
3:19-21 41
7:2-6 41
9:6 42
9:9 41
23:2,4 42
28:6 41

2 Samuel
2:1 41
12:1-12 41
21:1 42

1 Kings
3:5 41
4 42
8:8 42

Index of Subjects

Bibliography of items referred to

Botton, Alan de: *Religion for Atheists*; Hamish Hamilton
Bullinger, EW: *The Companion Bible;* Zondervan
Englishman's Greek Concordance of the New Testament; Bagster
Gray, Graham: *Disciples and Citizens: A Vision for Distinctive Living;*
    IVP
The Guardian
The Humanist
James, Oliver: *Affluenza;* Vermillion
Josephus: *Antiquities of the Jews*
Keyes, Richard: *Chameleon or Tribe? Recovering authentic Christian*
    Community; IVP
Messer, Neil: *Going by the Book: The Bible and Christian Ethics;*
    Canterbury Press
The Nativity; BBC TV
The New Bible Commentary Revised; IVP
The Passion; BBC TV
Penny, Michael: *40 Problems Passages;* OBT
Penny, Michael: *The Miracles of the Apostles;* OBT
Penny, Michael: *The Most Quoted Old Testament Prophecy;* OBT
The Times
Yuill, Chick: *Moving in the right circles*; IVP

More on the Will of God

The Will of God in the Bible and the 21st Century

William Henry and Michael Penny
(5 studies on 3 CDs)

Live recordings made at Open Bible Trust
Conferences. The five studies are:

- The Will of God in the Old Testament
- The Will of God for Jews in the Gospels and the Acts Period
- The Will of God for Jewish and Gentile Christians during the Acts
  Period and the Post-Acts Period
- The Will of God in the 21st Century – part 1
- The Will of God in the 21st Century – part 2

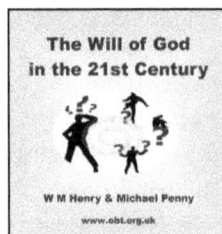

The Will of God
Michael Penny (4 studies on 2 DVDs)

A live recording of a *Search and See*
conference held in New Zealand.

- The Will of God in the Old Testament
- The Will of God in the Gospels and Acts Period
- The Will of God in the Post-Acts Period
- The Will of God today

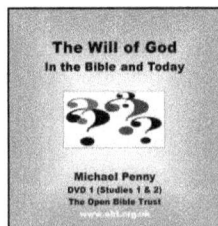

Please **visit www.obt.org.uk** for more information on these recordings.
Copies can be ordered from that website or from

The Open Bible Trust
Fordland Mount, Upper Basildon,
Reading, RG8 8LU, UK.

Further Reading

Following Philippians
William Henry & Michael Penny

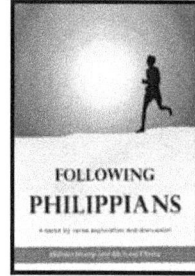

This book is much more than a commentary. It is a verse by verse exploration and discussion.

The authors first examine what a passage would have meant to the original first century Philippians, before seeking applications for 21st century Christians.

Each chapter of the book deals with a particular passage in Philippians in a number of ways.

- First, the *Big Issues* set out the main points of the passage.
- Then the passage is *Explored* with helpful insights into the historical setting of first century Philippi and the issues of that day.
- This is followed by a set of *Comprehensive Questions* on the passages,
- Next, the passage is *Discussed* in a manner which takes what has been learnt and discusses it, using it to direct light on to today's Christian experiences
- Each chapter concludes with a set of *Contemplative Questions* on each passage.

The result is a study guide to Philippians which balances well-researched historical information with practical lessons for today's Christian.

Reviews of this book can be seen on **www.obt.org.uk**

And copies can be ordered from that website or from

The Open Bible Trust
Fordland Mount, Upper Basildon,
Reading, RG8 8LU, UK.

40 Problem Passages
Michael Penny

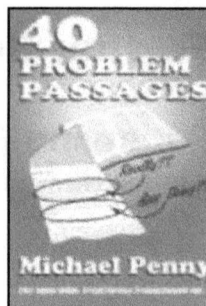

This book is a sequel to the author's earlier book *Approaching the Bible* It applies the principles set out there to *40 Problem Passages* from the Bible. In other words, it follows the advice given by Miles Coverdale. That advice was based on asking such questions as:

- "Who" were these words written to, or "Who" were they about?
- "Where" is this to take place?
- "When" was it written or "When" is it about?
- "What", precisely, is said?
- "Why" did God say it, do it, or will do it?

After asking such questions, we then will have a better understanding of the Bible and can "apply" that passage to our lives today.

There are far more that *40 Problem Passages* in the Bible! However, in this book the author not only solves these *40 Problem Passages*, he also equips the reader with a method by which many, many more problem passages can be understood.

Please **visit www.obt.org.uk** for more information on this book, including a list of the 40 passages considered.

Copies can be ordered from that website or from

The Open Bible Trust
Fordland Mount, Upper Basildon,
Reading, RG8 8LU, UK..